FIRE IN THE NORTH
The Minnesota Uprising and the Sioux War in Dakota Territory

Published by Hellgate Press
(An imprint of L&R Publishing, LLC)
PO Box 3531
Ashland, OR 97520
email: sales@hellgatepress.com

Editor: Harley B. Patrick
Book design: Michael Campbell
Cover design: L. Redding
Cover Illustration: "Indian attack on New Ulm, Minnesota, August 1862" by Henry Wellcome

ISBN: 978-1-55571-927-2

FIRE IN THE NORTH

*The Minnesota Uprising and the
Sioux War in Dakota Territory*

THOMAS D. PHILLIPS
REUBEN D. RIEKE

CONTENTS

PREFACE

THIS BOOK TELLS THE STORY of the major Indian war that exploded suddenly in the relatively settled region of south central Minnesota in 1862—a conflict that has come to be known as the Minnesota Uprising—and over the months that followed extended far west into the vast reaches of the Great Plains.

Interspersed in that broader tale is the story of three families brought together in the chaos of war by remarkable circumstances that bound them together in a connection that continues to the present day.

The authors are indebted to the Minnesota State Historical Society, several local newspapers, and, most of all, to the Rieke family whose records, personal correspondence, and eyewitness testimony contributed immeasurably to the telling of this story. In the interests of space and readability, we have followed recent convention and confined reference notes to directly quoted material.

The authors wish to express our appreciation to Caxton Press for allowing us to draw material from the work *Boots and Saddles: Military Leaders of the American West* for use in the portions of this book pertaining to John Pope, Henry Sibley, and Alfred Sully. Special thanks also go to Redge Johnson at

Images II for his outstanding work restoring the old photographs and creating the maps and diagrams displayed in this book and to Jeanne Kern and Kathleen Rutledge for their usual wisdom, wise counsel, and superb editing skills.

PROLOGUE

One of the largest and most costly of all of America's Indian wars began as a youthful dare. Before it was over, hundreds had been killed in a conflict that eventually extended over an immense portion of the central and western United States. Though often lost in the shadow cast by the cataclysmic events of the Civil War raging at the same time, the conflict along America's frontier witnessed the largest battle and the most casualties of any Indian war — as well as a mass hanging that surpassed anything similar in the nation's history.

ACTON TOWNSHIP: AUGUST 17, 1862

AUGUST 17 WAS A SUNDAY. It was a warm, clear day and many of the residents of the new state of Minnesota were enjoying a leisurely Sabbath. Nearing midday, four young Dakota Sioux warriors returning from an unsuccessful hunting trip passed by a farmstead in Acton Township in Meeker County about 80 miles west and a bit north of St. Paul. The four were from Rice Creek, a village 40 miles to the southwest. Noting some chicken eggs lying sheltered against a fence line not far from the farm house, they stopped to pilfer the nest. When one of the youths cautioned against taking the eggs, another questioned his bravery. His pride damaged, the youngster whose courage had been challenged claimed that he was not afraid and he would prove it by killing people who lived at the farm house.

Prodded to carry out his boast, he and the other three approached the dwelling, whose owner, Robinson Jones, and his wife ran a small store and post office on the farm's premises. The details of what followed remain a bit murky but there is some testimony that there may have been an initial period of benign interaction between the braves and the Jones family during which, by some accounts, the family refused the Indians' request for liquor.

Soon after, Jones, apparently sensing no threat, left to go to the nearby home of his brother-in-law, Howard Baker. The Indians followed. When all had arrived at Baker's place, there was some sort of marksmanship contest, an event not uncommon in the early settlements. Eventually, though—the circumstances are unclear—the four braves suddenly turned their weapons on Jones, killing him instantly. Jones' and Baker's wives, watching the shooting practice from the porch at Baker's house, then came under fire. Seeking to shield them, Baker jumped in front of the women and was killed by a shot to the chest. The braves then killed Mrs. Jones and a friend of the Bakers named Webster who was visiting the farm. As they were leaving, Clara Wilson, a young girl who had been adopted by the Jones family, stepped into the doorway of Jones's farm house. She too was slain.

When the fusillade was over, five people lay dead or dying on Minnesota soil. They would be the first of hundreds to follow.

Before the carnage was over, somewhere between 450 and 800 civilians would be killed with a figure of 757 being a recently cited estimate. In 1919, Minnesota newspaperman Marion P. Satterlee compiled a list 457 civilian and military deaths. Alexander Ramsey, governor of Minnesota at the time of the uprising, cited a figure of 500. President Abraham Lincoln referred to 800 dead in a public remark. Whatever the actual number, until exceeded by the tragic events of 9/11, the figure would represent the highest number of civilians killed by hostile action on American soil.

The conflagration spread quickly across the central and northern frontier. Eventually, much of Minnesota would be engulfed as would almost all of present day North and South Dakota and a sizable slice of eastern Montana. In varying degrees, parts of Wisconsin, Iowa, and Nebraska would be touched as well.

THE SEEDS OF CONFLICT

THOUGH THE KILLING of five settlers ignited the war that followed, the fuse had been simmering for many years. The Sioux had lived in southern Minnesota for generations, waging almost incessant war against the Chippewa tribe in a contest for land and hunting grounds. Treaties signed a decade earlier with the United States had left the Sioux with two agencies in Minnesota. Both were on the banks of the Minnesota River. The first, the Lower Sioux Agency, also called Redwood Falls, was on the south bank of the stream near the present-day city of the same name. The second, the Upper Sioux Agency, was 30 miles distant on the north side of the river near present-day Granite Falls.

The pacts — the Treaty of Traverse des Sioux, signed July 23, 1851, and the Treaty of Mendota, signed August 5, 1851 — each allotted areas of about 20 miles wide and 70 miles long to the Dakotas. The agreements involved different bands of the Greater Sioux nation. Through the Traverse des Sioux treaty, the Wahpeton and Sisseton bands of the Upper Sioux ceded lands in southern and western Minnesota Territory as well as parcels in Iowa and Dakota Territory in return for cash and annuities. The Treaty of Mendota, negotiated with the Mdewakanton and Wahpekute bands of the Lower

Sioux, brought much of the southwest corner of present-day Minnesota into the hands of the U.S .government. Altogether, through the treaties the Sioux relinquished about twenty-four million acres. Two years later the prime agricultural land was opened for settlement.

In 1858, under continuing pressure, the Sioux ceded additional land on the north side of the river. Left with reduced parcels of land not ideal for agriculture and inadequate in size and habitat to sustain a hunting culture, the Dakotas became increasingly dependent on treaty payments. In 1862, with the tribe increasingly under duress, the payments—normally distributed in late June or early July —were late once again.

From the outset, there had been periodic issues with the annuities promised to the tribes by the treaties. The money and goods were often late and the payment process was itself fraught with difficulties. Instead of timely compensation paid directly to them, the Sioux had agreed to treaty provisions that obligated them to purchase goods from local traders. The timing was such that the purchases typically occurred before the annuity payments arrived. Thus, when the money finally reached the reservations, much of it went straight to the traders in payment for the debts incurred by the tribesmen.

The Sioux complained, often with justification, about shoddy provisions, unscrupulous traders who plundered money and goods, and poor treatment by government representatives. On extreme occasions when government payments did not arrive, agents repossessed goods and implements they had provided to the Indians on credit and afterward sought payments for "debts in arrears" from the annuity moneys. When, in 1862, the annuity payments were yet again late in arriving, violence at the Upper Sioux Agency was only narrowly averted when on July 14 the agent, Thomas J. Galbraith—confronted by 500 Sioux warriors and a break-in at a warehouse—reluctantly agreed to issue limited amounts of food and supplies. On August 9, a second distribution defused another confrontation.

Conditions were equally tense at the Lower Sioux Agency where neither provisions of food nor extensions of credit to hungry Indians were immediately forthcoming. Andrew Jackson Myrick, a trader at the agency, an ill-tempered man already frustrated by being prohibited from using "trader's paper" that allowed vendors to be paid directly from annuity funds for what they were owed on credit, was heard to say "So far as I am concerned, if they are hungry, let them eat grass."

Very soon, Myrick would pay dearly for that remark.

As was often the case regarding areas that had been set aside for Native tribes, there was growing pressure on reservation land from increasing numbers of white immigrants. When the treaties were signed in 1851, the white population of Minnesota was about 6,000. Ten years later, it had risen to 200,000. Compounding the seeming perfect storm of misfortunes that befell the tribes was a series of crop failures that afflicted the Sioux agencies.

Added to these general factors were incidents more specific to time and place. In 1857, Inkpaduta, a renegade war chief of the Wahpekute band of Dakotas, and a small party of followers murdered more than 30 settlers and took four white women captive near Lake Okoboji, Iowa, an event that became known as the "Storm Lake Massacre." Soon after, the band crossed into Minnesota and killed several persons in Jackson County before escaping west into Dakota Territory where they easily eluded capture by the infantry units sent to apprehend them. Among the militant segments of the Sioux population, the government's failure to bring Inkpaduta to justice was seen as an indicator of the army's limited capability to combat fast-striking war parties.

Overshadowing all other considerations, however, was the on-going cataclysm on whose outcome the fate of the American nation depended. The Civil War had caused military forces to be withdrawn from the frontier garrisons, a fact well known to the Indians. At the same time, word was reaching the Sioux that the war was going badly for the Union. These factors provoked a variety of emotions among the tribes. One sentiment was to strike while the Army forces were weak and reeling. Another, apparently acute in 1862 when the payments were again late in arriving, was the considerable apprehension that the war was costing so much that there would be no money left to pay the tribe the promised annuity. A third, though apparently not as pervasive, was the fear that the rebels might indeed invade—or win—and enslave the Indians as they had the blacks. Conceivably, the latter notion may have led some to favor striking in an attempt to achieve some measure of quasi-independence—possible leverage in event of a Confederate victory.

THE OPPOSING SIDES

THE SIOUX NATION that was about to wage war against the white settlements was divided into two major, related bands. The largest, about 7,000 in number, was settled in groups along the Minnesota River. The second, with a population of about 3,000–4,000, roamed farther west in Dakota Territory. Not all of either group, it must be said, were eager to go to war. There existed a sizable peace element — "friendlies" as they were called — within the tribe that would later play an influential role as the conflict drew to an end. The combined assemblage was believed to have about 1,500 to 2,000 warriors readily available.

While a chief named Little Crow was to a degree the presumptive overall leader, the nature of his authority was — as with the organization of the tribal groups — rather loose. The bands operated semi-independently; there was little resembling a formal chain of command. Decisions were made by consensus and to a considerable extent adherence to them was voluntary. The authority of war leaders was often based on reputation, personal qualifications or some form of moral suasion.

Though notoriously ill-disciplined, Sioux braves were known as fearsome warriors. War was inherent in the tribe's culture. Conflicts of varying severity, scope, and size were a near-perpetual feature of tribal existence before their days on the reservation. Status within a group was often accorded based on success in combat. Tenacious and aggressive, the Sioux would pose formidable opponents for the thinly-spread Army units initially sent to oppose them.

When the uprising began, Army forces in the region—many of whom would soon be withdrawn for Civil War duty and replaced by local volunteers—were primarily garrisoned at four locations. Two were in Dakota Territory: Fort Abercrombie, on the Red River a half-mile east of present-day Abercrombie, North Dakota; and Fort Randall, on the southwest bank of the Missouri River about 45 miles west of present-day Yankton, South Dakota. The remaining posts were in Minnesota. Fort Ridgely was 12 miles northwest of New Ulm on the Minnesota River. Fort Ripley was on the Mississippi River about 40 miles north of St. Cloud. Altogether, the combined garrisons housed 879 soldiers. A third post in Minnesota, Fort Snelling, was at the confluence of the Minnesota and Mississippi rivers in Hennepin County. Deactivated in 1858, the post was leased back to the federal government during the Civil War. Although the fort maintained a small garrison, it was used primarily as an induction and training center for enlistees in the Union Army.

At the war's outset, Sioux forces were primarily divided into two war parties. One, operating farthest south, would fight major battles at Fort Ridgely and New Ulm. That force would eventually be involved in a series of raids and skirmishes such as a noted encounter at Birch Coulee. The second band would raid Minnesota's northern counties and attack Fort Abercrombie. Their goal was to exterminate white settlers in the area between the Dakota border and the Mississippi River.

THE BATTLEGROUND

TWO PROMINENT FEATURES mark the landscape over which the fighting raged during the blood-soaked days that would follow. The first, the Minnesota River Valley, is unusual in its size and depth. Created thousands of years ago by receding glaciers, it is not at all like the shallow depressions that trace the streams on most American prairies. In Minnesota, the glaciers tore at the earth over the millennia carving a valley hundreds of feet deep and several miles across from rim to rim. Steep banks, often 10 to 20 feet high, straddle the wide stream that typically runs about 6 to 10 feet in depth. Though the river was not deep enough for large commercial traffic, in the 19th century shallow draft boats carried settlers and supplies to the recently chartered city of New Ulm. Twenty miles farther upstream Fort Ridgely also became a major destination after its construction in the mid-1850s. Ultimately, steam boats went even farther—20 miles to the Lower Sioux Agency and 70 more miles to the Upper Sioux Agency. Thus, the waterway was significant to the lives of Natives and settlers alike. When the spreading conflagration shut down river traffic and other means of commerce the effects were felt throughout the region.

Elsewhere, the departing ice scraped the soil leaving it relatively flat, exposing some of the most fertile black soil on the continent. Thousands of small bodies of water called sloughs were also left behind. Nourished by the abundant supply of water, the prairie formed a lush, grassy landscape in which plants, waterfowl, and wildlife flourished. Bison, deer, elk and other large mammals ranged the landscape in seemingly countless numbers. The sloughs, surrounded by bulrushes, cattails, and reed grass, provided homes for muskrats, mink, weasels, and ducks. Muskrats were particularly prized for their meat and for the pelts that Natives and settlers alike sold to supplement their incomes.

Unlike the dryer soil farther west on the Great Plains, the ground in southern Minnesota seemed capable of growing almost anything. Crops of grains—oats, wheat, and barley—and corn thrived and an extraordinary variety of nuts and wild berries carpeted the landscape. In many ways, the setting seemed ideal to the settlers who arrived in ever-increasing numbers and to the Natives who fondly recalled the time when they roamed without boundaries across the prairie. Neither the settlers with their hopes nor the Natives with their memories would surrender the land or their visions easily.

THE RIEKE FAMILY

THE RIEKE FAMILY began migrating to the United States in 1853. First to arrive from their ancestral home in northwest Prussia were the two oldest sons of Johann Friederich, a miller in the small town of Osnabruck, and his wife Maria Gertrude. Fred, the oldest, came in 1853 followed two years later by George. Both initially settled in Portsmouth, Ohio, where they worked in the steel mills and mining industry. The two boys saved their money and over the next few years brought the entire Rieke family, their parents, six brothers and three sisters, to the United States.

The Rieke's presence in Ohio was likely never intended to be permanent. If not initially part of their plan, acquisition of land farther west in the growing nation rather quickly drew their attention as word of opportunities and fertile soil along the frontier filtered back to Ohio. Their choice of location seems to have been between Kansas and Minnesota. Because of the pro- versus anti-slavery, bushwhacker versus jayhawker, disputes in what became known as "Bleeding Kansas," the Riekes chose Minnesota. In the days prior to the Homestead Act, federal preemption law permitted the filing of claims for a quarter section (160 acres) and payment of fees at a government land office. Land was available for as little as $1.25 an acre. The affordable price plus the presence of sizable numbers of German-speaking settlers probably made the choice of Minnesota fairly easy.

The Riekes began their further migration in the spring of 1859. Two brothers having already married and with infants at home to care for, it was decided that George and Victor, both unmarried, would make the initial journey and prepare for the later arrival of the extended family. George, 25, and Victor, 23, boarded a steamboat near Portsmouth in March, traveling first down the Ohio to the Mississippi River and then on to St. Louis. At St. Louis, they took another steamer to St. Paul before heading up the Minnesota River. It seems likely that they would have stopped at New Ulm before continuing up the valley where available land was more plentiful.

Passing through Fort Ridgely they met by chance John Buechro, a recently discharged veteran who told them about his homestead five miles away on Rush Lake (now called Mud Lake). As Buechro described it, the east side of the lake, protected from prairie fires, had ample stands of trees for construction and fire wood. The soil itself was rich and black. The lake provided a nearby source of water and teemed with fish and ducks. With land available near Buechro's property, they decided to take a homestead on the southeast corner of the lake. On July 3, 1859, George Rieke filed papers for the first Rieke homestead in America. The deed for the property was later signed by Abraham Lincoln and became one of George's most prized possessions.

Cash poor for a time due to the price of their steamer passage, George and Victor trapped muskrats and sold their pelts in New Ulm to supplement their income (a practice that continued for generations). Eventually, that revenue and the produce from the farm enabled them to bring the entire family to Minnesota. They also purchased a team of oxen, a plow, and other essentials. A short time later they began supplying Fort Ridgely with firewood and selling hay for the soldiers' horses.

At the homestead site, the brothers first constructed a lean-to to provide temporary shelter while a more permanent sod house was built. With the arrival of the rest of the family the following summer (1860), the sod house became the residence of the parents, Friederich and Gertrude. The "soddy" later saw service as a stable for oxen until wooden facilities could be built. Soon an impressive 16- by 24- foot log house was completed. The house and all of its furniture were built by hand without the use of nails.

Until they settled in Minnesota, the Riekes knew little about Indians and had no contact with the Sioux. They quickly developed a reputation for friendly interaction with local tribesmen. Deeply religious, the Riekes treated the Indians charitably and were scrupulously fair in their trade transactions with them.

All of the family learned rudiments of the Sioux language and to a greater extent than most of their neighbors were able to communicate with tribal members. When cold weather approached, the Riekes left the door to their home unlocked. Sioux hunting parties passing the house on their return from the Upper Sioux Agency would often enter the house after the Riekes were in bed, sleep on the floor near the fireplace, and leave the next morning before the family got up.

The depth of the relationship between the family and the Sioux is evidenced by a special gift given the family by a tribal elder. The memento is an ornate pipestone peace pipe, carved from a quarry near present-day Pipestone, Minnesota. The soft red stone was considered sacred, a gift to the Indians from the Great Spirit.

THE LAMMERS FAMILY

LIKE THE RIEKES, the Lammers family had migrated first to Portsmouth, Ohio, from their home in Prussia. There is no evidence that the families knew one another in Europe, but in Ohio they became neighbors and friends before eventually being linked by marriage. In 1857 or 1858, Fred, the oldest Rieke son, married Wilhelmine, the oldest Lammers child. After the birth of their first child, in 1860, they moved with the rest of the family to Minnesota, settling seven miles downstream from Fort Ridgely, not far from Rush Lake and the rest of the Rieke family.

Wilhelmine's brother Wilhelm married Sophie Schweer, probably in 1855. In 1862, Wilhelm decided to join his eldest sister and her husband Fred Rieke in Minnesota. Wilhelm, Sophie and their two sons, ages six and one and a half, arrived at Fort Ridgely in early May. The area surrounding the fort was being rapidly filled by the influx of settlers so Wilhelm had to go 24 miles upstream to find open land. The family eventually settled in Flora Township, near the Kietzmanns, fellow emigres of German descent; Wilhelm quickly built a cabin, cleared some land, and planted wheat, oats, and barley. When the four young Sioux killed Robinson Jones and others a few months later, Sophie was expecting her third child.

THE APPROACHING STORM

THE RIEKE FAMILY archives contain an intriguing reference to an unusual event that occurred a few days before the uprising began. When the Riekes first arrived in the area in 1859, the region was sparsely settled. Indians mixed freely with the newcomers—who had quickly learned the Sioux language—establishing a cordial relationship notable for the depth of personal friendships between Dakota tribesmen and family members.

By the summer of 1862, the Rieke brothers had negotiated a contract to supply hay to Fort Ridgely. The exact date is uncertain but sometime in the week preceding the outbreak, George Rieke and three of his brothers were at the work site when they were approached by perhaps as many as 200 Sioux warriors on horseback. The braves asked the Riekes for bread, pork, and tobacco. This was not, in itself, an unusual request. The Riekes were known for their generosity and, as was typical of them, they supplied what they could spare. This time, however, instead of expressing their gratitude and immediately devouring the food, the warriors responded harshly, throwing the food on the ground, spitting at it, and trampling it into the earth.

The undertones of menace, though muted at the time, must have been fairly widespread. In reminiscences written years later, Minnie Buce Carrigan, whose family resided near Buffalo Lake, recalled a similar puzzling change in the Sioux's behavior in the days prior to the uprising. The relationship between the Indians and the Buce family had always been cordial. Indeed, members of the tribe were frequent houseguests in the Buce home. Rather suddenly, however, "the Sioux became disagreeable and ill-natured. They seldom visited us and when they met us passed by coldly and sullenly and often without speaking."

After leaving the Rieke's worksite, the Sioux party then proceeded to Fort Ridgely, where they again demanded food. The post commander, Captain John S. Marsh, was away from the fort at the time. Sergeant John Jones, a veteran noncommissioned officer, was in charge when the Indians arrived. Jones provided the Sioux with food from the fort's commissary supplies. The party then asked to conduct a dance inside the post compound. Puzzled by the Indians' behavior and skeptical of their intentions Jones, with only 25 or so soldiers at hand, refused the request. Sometime during the parley, he trained one of the fort's howitzers on the assembled warriors and asked them to leave. The Sioux eventually complied with the order and departed.

Although there had been periodic flashpoints between settlers and tribesmen during the preceding months, most had subsided or been defused by actions such as that taken as recently as August 9 by Thomas Galbraith at the Upper Sioux Agency who, in the absence of promised annuity payments, provided members of the tribe with food. Thus, the Indians' actions, while out of character, were apparently not viewed with undue alarm.

The uprising exploded a few days later. When it came, its size, scope, and intensity were on a scale that far surpassed anything previously experienced in wars along the American frontier.

LITTLE CROW

WHEN THE FOUR young braves reached their Rice Creek encampment, they immediately reported what they had done. The series of tribal meetings that followed that evening eventually involved Little Crow, who though not universally admired within the tribe, was perhaps the only influential leader who had credibility throughout the Dakota Sioux population.

About 50 years old at the time, Little Crow was slender, had a sharply pointed nose and direct, piercing eyes. Both wrists were deformed, having been broken during fights in his youth. While not a strong friend of the white man, he had been to Washington D.C. to participate in treaty negotiations and understood the looming strength and endless numbers of white immigrants who would inevitably push against the Sioux homeland. Much that he had seen in his journeys had impressed him — enormous cities, technology, weapons, and the sheer power of the national government. Perhaps most of all, he had been struck by the size of the restless white population. He was known to have said that killing one white would result in ten more taking his place.

Nevertheless, though the action of the four braves had not been premeditated, Little Crow and many other leaders of the assembled bands believed that the killings would surely disrupt already frayed relations past the point of no return. In their view the die had been cast. They would, it was decided, wage a pre-emptive war—and it would begin the following day.

AUGUST 18: THE TERROR BEGINS

THE SIOUX WASTED little time in launching hostilities. On August 18, in the morning of the day following the go to war decision, Little Crow led a war party that swept through the Lower Sioux Agency. One of the first to be killed was Andrew Jackson Myrick—he of the "let them eat grass" comment. Myrick was caught as he tried to escape through a second-floor window. Days later, his body was found with grass stuffed into his mouth.

The agency consisted of several buildings—stores, a blacksmith shop, saw mill, doctor's office, and a school, among others. Many of the structures were quickly set afire by the war party. In the smoke and confusion that followed, 47 settlers managed to escape using a nearby ferry to cross the river. Nonetheless, several settlers—the most commonly cited figure is 13—were killed in the attack and several more were killed while attempting to flee. The Sioux took 10 prisoners. They would be the first of many more that would follow.

By now alerted to the looming danger—news of the raid on the agency reached Fort Ridgely at mid-morning of that day—authorities began dispatching forces in an attempt to quell the unrest before it exploded beyond the limits of local control. The first countermove met with disaster. At Fort Ridgely, a hurriedly assembled force of local militia and soldiers from the fort set out for the agency. Within hours, they were surprised by a well-conceived ambush. At least 20 soldiers — many credible sources cite a figure of 24 — were killed.

That disaster, at a river crossing known as Redwood Ferry, was only a precursor to the many horrific events that would rage on unabated throughout the day. Entire townships — Milford, Leavenworth and Sacred Heart among them — were surrounded, burned to the ground, and their populations systematically annihilated.

The slaughter at Milford Township, a short distance west of New Ulm, was representative of many inflicted on farms and settlements scattered through the region. Sioux raiders struck the unsuspecting settlers in early morning. The scene afterward was one of complete devastation. Within a one-mile radius, 53 people — members of 10 Minnesota families — lay dead or dying. Soon after, four members of a small wagon train were killed.

The depredations were only beginning. Upriver from New Ulm another wagon party was attacked. All of the men were killed and the women were taken as prisoners. Almost 30 more were killed at Beaver Falls.

These murders added to an already ghastly toll. Large numbers had already been killed at the Lower Sioux Agency during Little Crow's attack. At Redwood Ferry, several had died even before the column from Fort Ridgely reached the area. After killing the ferry operator, the Sioux set an ambush utilizing cover on both sides of the river. As the day progressed they killed others who stumbled into their trap, including members of a caravan carrying unarmed military enlistees on their way to Civil War service. Those who managed to escape raced away raising the alarm and sowing additional panic.

Terror spread through the settlements. The day brought mixed news of horrific deaths, mutilations, fleeing families, miraculous escapes, and towns and farms engulfed in infernos. Isolated homesteads were especially vulnerable. Most were attacked without warning. Grisly tales abetted the panic. Near Lake Shetek in Murray County, the Sioux caught settler families seeking shelter in a swamp—a place forever after called "Slaughter Slough"—killing at least 15 and wounding several more. Twenty or more communities were attacked before nightfall brought a momentary end to the carnage. In a macabre scene that extended for miles, the night sky was lit with clouds of smoke and flames from burning farms and villages that dotted the horizon.

August 18 was a day of abject horror throughout the Minnesota River Valley. No one was safe. Families were attacked inside their homes and outside in their fields. Dozens were killed as they attempted to flee as Sioux raiders ranged unchecked across southwestern Minnesota.

In a pattern that would continue through the uprising, the first white captives were taken. Eventually more than 200—almost all women and children—would be held prisoner, and used as leverage as the uprising continued. The drama surrounding the captive population would, in a major way, influence the end game that eventually brought the Minnesota portion of the conflict to a close.

One of the many ironies of the Sioux Uprising of 1862—like most others, this one had major implications—was that at about the same time the column from Fort Ridgely was perishing at Redwood Ferry, the annuity payments arrived. They were two months late. Had they arrived perhaps even a day sooner, they quite likely would have prevented the war.

The $71,000 in payments had reached St. Paul on August 16. The money was then carried to Fort Ridgely in a stagecoach that by some stroke of fate made it unscathed through the surrounding chaos. The money was first kept in the officers' quarters, a stone building, or by one less credited account buried at least temporarily on the grounds for safekeeping until the crisis was over.

Fueled by their successes on the 18th, the Sioux planned a series of strikes in the days ahead. The first was to be carried out the next day. The target was New Ulm. The city was not the objective originally planned for that day; the Sioux had initially intended the strike to fall on Fort Ridgely. As preparations were being made, disagreements among the Sioux—some believed the fort might be too heavily defended—caused the Dakotas to shift their objective to New Ulm, thought by many to offer a more promising prospect.

This, too, was an irony. On the 19th, the place was only lightly defended. In fact, a portion of the already small garrison had been sent to New Ulm.

By now refugees fortunate enough to escape the killings had begun streaming into the city. At New Ulm, leaders formed a posse to scour the countryside, seeking to rescue survivors. Couriers were sent racing to nearby towns to seek assistance. Convinced that an attack was inevitable, townspeople began erecting the defenses that would play a major role in the drama that would soon follow.

PERILOUS JOURNEYS

FOR THE RIEKES, the morning had begun like most other August work days. They were busy with the business they had established, cutting and delivering hay to Fort Ridgely. Working from a temporary camp to support their haying operations, they cut hay with a hand sickle and dried it in the sun before taking it to the fort. Early on the 18th, they pitchforked loads of hay into two wagons, hitched teams of oxen to them, and brothers George and Adam hauled the hay to the fort. They arrived at the post in mid-morning, unloaded the wagons and received their payment.

As they were preparing to leave, possibly around ten o'clock, a German settler who lived several miles farther upstream hurried into the fort with the first news of the Sioux uprising. The brothers learned of the deaths of several people at the Lower Sioux Agency and heard the farmer's report that the killing rampage was spreading rapidly. George and Adam left immediately for the hay camp with two wagons, where they picked up their father, brothers Victor and August, and sister Mary. After bringing them back to the relative safety of the fort, they took a single wagon and left for the homestead on Mud Lake to gather up the remaining members of the family—their mother, brothers

Henry and Herman, and sisters Lasetta and Wilhelmine. At some point in the journey they retrieved their neighbor, Mrs. John Buechro, as they made their way without incident back to the fort.

Victor Rieke had remained at the fort while George and Adam were gathering the family. As dozens—soon to be hundreds—of refugees poured in to the fort, the water supply was already becoming a major concern. Unable, or unwilling, to spare a rifleman from his woefully under-manned post, Lt. Thomas Gere, in command at the time, asked Victor to take the wagon left by George and Adam and fetch a supply of water from Fort Ridgely Creek. Victor did so, going alone to the stream. After filling his wagon with several barrels of water, he headed back to the fort. The post was already beginning to be threatened at various points by Sioux warriors. In his later years, Victor described the sight and sound of arrows whizzing past him and his oxen as he made his perilous way back to the fort.

Meanwhile, Fred Rieke and his family, who had settled a few miles from Mud Lake and the main Rieke homestead, headed east to the town of St. Peter. It was a fortunate deci-sion. The town was not struck during the uprising, although had Fort Ridgely and New Ulm fallen, St. Peter would undoubtedly have been a Sioux target.

SOPHIE LAMMERS

WHEN NEWS of the massacres reached the Lammers household, they made hurried preparations to leave for the nearest safe haven—Fort Ridgely— 24 long and desperate miles away. Sophie's husband, Wilhelm, quickly hitched their oxen to the family's wagon, threw in some supplies and headed first to the Kietzmann farm. Eventually, 13 families gathered at the Kietzmann homestead. That evening the combined group of families—some 60 people in all traveling in 11 wagons pulled by oxen—started for Fort Ridgely. After they had travelled all night over rough prairie grass and marginal tracks, sunrise found them still several miles from safety.

Shortly after sunup the caravan was intercepted by eight Sioux warriors. After a considerable parley, the Indians convinced the settlers that it was Chippewa tribesmen—not Sioux warriors —who were on the warpath. Accepting the Sioux's version of events, the settlers turned around and began the trek back to their homesteads. Later that day they were overtaken by a large band of Sioux led by Little Crow. An eyewitness account describes what happened next. The adult men and women were lined up in a single file with Wilhelm Lammers placed next to Sophie. A Sioux warrior then came down the line shooting each person in the head. He stood next to Wilhelm and killed him. He then moved beside Sophie, placed the gun to her head and pulled the trigger. The bullet was a dud that made only a loud clicking noise without firing. The Sioux considered the misfire to be a sign that the woman should not be killed. At least for the moment, Sophie and her two young children were spared.

AUGUST GLUTH

TWO YOUNG BOYS traveling with the Lammers party were the only other survivors. One of the two was August Gluth, a precocious 12-year-old. After migrating from Germany, his family had eventually settled on a farm near Milford, Minnesota. Conditions were difficult. Their land was not especially productive and for two consecutive years the weather was not conducive to raising crops. There being several mouths to feed, young August set out on his own, moving from farm to farm up the valley in the general direction of Fort Ridgely. Earning his keep with odd jobs at several farmsteads or subsisting on wild berries or handouts from settler families, he often slept under the stars. His wanderings eventually took him 40 miles from home to a farm near Beaver Falls where he found a job herding cattle and oxen.

When word of the uprising reached the family August was staying with, they hitched their oxen, gathered a few cattle, and began moving towards the fort, stopping first at the Kietzmann residence where they joined the Lammers party and others who had gathered there. When the Indians intercepted the caravan the next day, the entire party except for Sophie Lammers and her two children, and the two boys, were killed.

It was August's skill with oxen and horses that saved his life.

Oxen were very difficult animals to manage. It was immediately obvious to the Indians that August knew how to handle them. He was also an adept horseman and rather quickly was given the additional chore of tending to Little Crow's prized ponies. His captor would prove to be a harsh and demanding master.

While August was being taken prisoner, elsewhere on that long day his family's home in Milford was attacked. John Gluth, his 22-year-old brother, was shot to death. A younger brother was wounded. August's parents and remaining children fled to New Ulm where they survived the heavy fighting that would rage in and around the city. The family's tragedy did not end with the death of one son, the wounding of another, and the capture of a third. They would soon receive word that another son, Fred, had been killed in action while serving with the Union Army.

JOHN OTHER DAY

ALTHOUGH AUGUST 18 would be a day of almost unmitigated horror throughout south central Minnesota, interspersed among hours of terror were moments of incredible bravery, some of which came from unexpected sources.

John Other Day was a full-blooded Sioux. In 1858, he had married a white woman and converted to Christianity. He and his wife lived on a farm near the Lower Sioux Agency.

Sometime before the attack occurred, Other Day learned of it and raced to warn as many as he could. At the Lower Sioux Agency, he hid 62 people in a warehouse while the attack swirled all around him. Amid burning buildings, shooting, and looting, he stood guard outside the building to protect the people inside. The next day, he led all 62—men, women, and children—on a three-day journey to safety at Cedar City. The Sioux burned his home and ruined his fields in retaliation.

Later in the war, Other Day scouted for the army during the Wood Lake campaign.

Other Day's was not the only act of valor performed in aid of settlers. Struck by the Ree, a Sioux chief, sent his warriors to protect nearby white residents from harm.

When placed in context with the almost uncountable atrocities and acts of violence committed by other tribesmen, the actions of Sioux such as Other Day and Struck by the Ree evidenced the widely contrasting attitudes held within the tribe regarding the white population and the war in general.

E.W. EARLE

THE STORY of E.W. Earle, a slender, brown-haired teenager and his family is representative of the circumstances faced by many settlers across south central Minnesota as the horrific hours of August 18 passed.

The Earle farm was on Beaver Creek in Renville County, six miles from the Lower Sioux Agency and about 18 miles from Fort Ridgely. Though initially puzzled by the sound of Indian drums on the night of August 17 and by the unusual behavior of a few Sioux braves the following morning—some came into the Earle's house and demanded guns, others wanted horses—the family was not at first unduly concerned. Suspicions grew during the day as E.W. later interacted with a group of young Dakotas, whose behavior towards him seemed strained and on the part of some, uncharacteristically belligerent. The family's apprehensions reached the point of alarm when a neighbor named Wichman raced by to tell them that the Sioux were on a killing rampage, slaughtering any whites they came across.

After rounding up their horses, the Earle family left for Fort Ridgely, forming a caravan with 27 others—men, women, children, and two infants—from the immediate area. They had only five weapons among them and not enough powder or ammunition to reload after firing a single shot.

Within five minutes, 16 Indians crossed the road ahead of them while three more closed in from behind. All were well armed. Eventually, the Earle party was surrounded. A member of the group, a neighbor named Henderson who spoke the Sioux language, attempted to negotiate. Henderson refused the Dakotas' request to give up the group's guns, but in return for a promise of safe passage, gave the Indians wagons and horses, forcing the Earle contingent to pull a buggy carrying Mrs. Henderson and two little girls by hand.

Some time later, the Indians struck as the party headed down a small knoll. The buggy carrying the Henderson family was quickly engulfed. Hopelessly outgunned, the rest of the party tried to race away as the Sioux killed Mrs. Henderson and the two children as well as a man named Wedge who stayed with the group and attempted to assist Mr. Henderson in defending the family. Though wounded, Henderson ran through a rain of fire somehow reaching the rest of the Earle party. Separated from his father and mother, a small boy who could not keep up was quickly killed by the Sioux. Another member of the group, wounded in the knee, was also caught then shot to death at close range.

Later in the day, one of E.W.'s brothers was killed while coming to the defense of his father who had temporarily separated himself from the rest of the party. As the hours passed, E.W.'s mother and other women were taken captive. When a pregnant woman unable to maintain the pace was left behind, she was surprisingly well treated by the Dakotas. Members of the Earle party later conjectured that at least some of the Sioux were determined to capture women and children.

Still the day was not over. Late in the afternoon with Indians all around, while momentarily out of view crossing over the top of a hill, E.W. rolled out of sight down the slope. Hiding through the night in tall grass, he narrowly escaped capture by warriors whose search took them within a few feet of his hiding place. When he awoke the next morning he set out on a circuitous route toward Fort Ridgely. Later in the day he stumbled across an army patrol that took him to safety at the post.

DEATH ON THE PRAIRIE

BEFORE THE DAY was over, the entire region would be ravaged by attacks whose number and violence were almost beyond comprehension. Horrors such as those inflicted on E.W. Earle's family were commonplace throughout a long and bloody day marked by mass killings and hostage taking occasionally interspersed with near-miraculous escapes. About five miles west, a story similar to Earle's unfolded near the residence of Louis Thiele.

Thiele was a native of Berlin, Germany, who had come to America in 1856 after the death of his first wife. Thiele settled first in Wisconsin, remarried, and then in 1858 moved to Renville County where he established a homestead in the extreme southeast corner of Flora Township.

Although the exact circumstances are not recorded, Thiele was taking his family to Fort Ridgely, seeking shelter there, when they were attacked by a Sioux war party. Within moments his wife and four-year-old son were killed. Thiele jumped from his wagon and raced under fire to some nearby woods, somehow managing to avoid capture. Subsisting mainly on corn and wild plums, he eventually made his way to Fort Ridgely where he and Earle, who had also escaped almost certain death, were among the civilians who took up arms in defense of the fort.

Perhaps because there were few or no survivors — or because those who did survive were immediately engaged in life-sustaining endeavors — not many direct accounts of attacks on settler farms exist. One of the most detailed was written years later by Minnie Buce Carrigan who described events at her home near Buffalo Lake where she lived with her parents Gottfried and Wilhemina and five siblings.

When the family heard shots and screams from a nearby farm, Minnie's older brother August was sent to investigate. He found the entire family, the Roslers, had been slain. While Wilhelmina went to find her husband who was putting up hay the children were told to hide in a cornfield south of the house.

Then, in Minnie's words:

> *We had hardly reached the cornfield when the Indians came whooping and yelling around the west side of the field… We sat down and they passed us so closely that it was strange they did not see us. They rushed into our house and we went on. Looking back we saw them throwing out the featherbeds and other articles. We reached the south side of the field safely and father and mother were already there. I think we would have been safe there at least for a time, but father taking the baby from Augusta, started out on the open prairie. Mother took Caroline from me and tried to stop father, but it was useless. The terrible circumstances must have unbalanced his mind, naturally being very nervous.*

The Indians cleared out of our house and… as they were passing a little corner of the timber one of them saw father and uttered a wicked piercing yell. It was but a moment when the whole band, about 20 men and some women, were upon us. My father began talking to the foremost Indians. My brother has told me that father asked them to take all his property but to let him and his family go. But… the Indian then leveled his double barreled shotgun and fired both barrels at him. He dropped the baby—she was killed—and running a few yards down the hill, fell on his face, dead. The same Indian then went to where my mother had sat down beside a stone with little Caroline in her lap, reloaded his gun and deliberately fired upon them both. She did not speak or utter a sound, but fell over dead. Caroline gave one little scream and a gasp or two and all was over with her. The cry rang in my ears for years afterward. My father was thirty-three and my mother thirty years of age when they were killed…

Minnie, seven years old, and her surviving siblings August and Amelia, twelve and four years old, respectively, were taken captive. They were held prisoner at Camp Release until set free several weeks later.

NEW ULM: AUGUST 19

LOCATED AT THE confluence of the Minnesota and Cottonwood Rivers, New Ulm had been chartered only recently, in 1856, just two years prior to Minnesota's achieving statehood. Blessed by its excellent location and the industriousness of the German immigrants who settled there, the town had thrived. Two years later, in 1858, it already boasted two general stores, a grocery store, a saloon, a hotel, a sawmill, two grist mills, several blacksmith shops, and a newspaper. By 1862, it had grown to nearly a thousand inhabitants and about 300 buildings. Now, in one horrific week, the town would be abandoned and most of those structures would be utterly destroyed, burned to the ground.

Sunrise of August 19 revealed a blood-soaked vista across the fields and valleys near the town. Attacks throughout the day would add further to the toll as the scale of the uprising became increasingly apparent. Raids in Kandiyohi County, Lake Shetek, and numerous other locations would kill many more before the end of the day.

Little Crow had the Sioux on the move by sunup. With 400 warriors he headed toward Fort Ridgely which, along with New Ulm, he regarded as the keys to victory in the conflict.

Then, for reasons not apparent at the time, the Sioux stopped near the fort, their presence visible to its inhabitants. Just out of range of the defenders' weapons, the Sioux inexplicably halted. They had stopped to talk. The focus of their parley, which lasted for hours, was a debate about strategy. Though uncertain about the fort's strength, Little Crow favored attacking Fort Ridgely. Others in the contingent, perhaps believing that New Ulm was a more lucrative target and likely less strongly defended, argued in favor of striking the city instead. In the end, contentions caused the group to split. Little Crow, with the bulk of the party, returned to the Sioux encampment. Meanwhile, the New Ulm faction, about 100 strong, moved toward the city.

Since the first refugees, relaying harrowing tales of atrocities and mass killings, began flowing into New Ulm, the town had been the scene of frenetic activity. Guided by Brown County Sheriff Charles Roos and Jacob Nix, a veteran of the German Army, the citizens of New Ulm began preparing to meet the terror about to be thrust upon them.

An area in the center of town about three blocks long and two blocks wide was established as the main defensive position. About 50 feet from the buildings, barricades were constructed enclosing the inner defensive area. These bastions, put together using any available material including earthen embankments and overturned wagons, allowed observers inside the buildings to identify areas under threat and shift forces to meet attacks that came from scattered points along the perimeter. Holes were chipped in exterior walls to create firing ports in the buildings.

By the time the first attack came at about three o'clock in the afternoon perhaps as many as 2,000 refugees were clustered inside the hastily constructed compound with wagons, livestock, and the few possessions they had managed to salvage. All were crammed inside an area of six square blocks. Many of the noncombatants were placed inside brick buildings to afford them additional protection. Possibly less than 100 armed men—some scholars say only about 40—were available to face the initial Sioux onslaught. Many possessed only shotguns. Others armed with clubs or axes, some even with pitchforks, helped man the barricades or protected doorways, shielding the refugees crowded inside the buildings.

New Ulm was not an easy place to defend. In 1862, most of the houses were on a lower plateau, the first of two that rose like steps above the Minnesota River. A ravine separated the two terraces and a heavily wooded area capped the higher bluff. Both afforded ample cover to attackers.

Indeed, the first attack came from the higher plateau west of the town. At about 3:00 PM, a mass of warriors, initially most of the 100 who formed the war party, swept down the bluff. Brought quickly under fire, most dismounted and continued to force their way down the slope, halting periodically to exchange fire as they made their way toward New Ulm's barricades and outlying buildings.

Many who assaulted the barricades became entangled in close, hand-to-hand combat with defenders who hurried to meet them. Others occupied buildings outside the main perimeter and used doors, windows, and porches as firing positions. Before the day was over, many of the buildings outside the barricades were looted and several were on fire.

As fighting continued, the city's defenders shifted men from place to place to confront assaults that threatened to overwhelm the town's defenders. Nix, among others, led sorties outside the barricades to clear the Sioux from structures whose fields of fire posed particular hazards for the struggling defenders.

At times fighting raged from house to house, occasionally taking place inside buildings that were already on fire. Sharp attacks from the Sioux continued, mostly coming from the north and west, as the day wore on. During the next few hours, small groups of armed volunteers periodically made their way to New Ulm to assist in the town's defense. The largest cadre, about 15 men led by Lorenzo Boardman, the sheriff of Nicollet County, fought their way through to the city in early afternoon. The company immediately joined the fight along and outside the barricades.

At about the same time that Boardman's group joined the fighting, a powerful thunderstorm swept through the area. Lightning illuminated the scene as a torrential downpour doused the fires that had raged unchecked in dozens of the town's buildings. Shortly after, apparently swayed by the advent of the storm and the arrival of the Boardman and other groups, the Sioux broke off the attack.

Fighting that day had been intense with little quarter given by either side. Six of New Ulm's defenders had been killed and five more wounded, including Jacob Nix, whose leadership of several forays outside the barricades had helped anchor the city's defense. The extent of Sioux losses has never been determined, although townspeople observed several bodies being carried away as the Sioux departed.

New Ulm had survived August 19. A sterner and more ominous test would follow four days later.

FORT RIDGELY: AUGUST 20

FORT RIDGELY is situated high on a bluff on a projection formed by the Minnesota River to the south and a creek which enters it at a sharp angle from the north and east. The bluff is steep and at the time of the battle was surrounded by areas that were heavily timbered.

The fort had been the original target for a massive strike intended by the Sioux for August 19, when disputes between competing factions of the war party had disrupted plans. While the majority of the group went home, the remaining cadre launched a strong attack against the city of New Ulm.

One of the issues that dissuaded the war party from attacking the fort was the conviction among at least some influential leaders that the fort was strongly defended. In reality, that was not the case. The place was only minimally garrisoned with 78 soldiers when the war began in earnest on August 18. Conditions quickly became even more dire when at mid-morning, Captain Marsh, the fort's commanding officer, took 46 men to reconnoiter conditions at the Lower Sioux Agency after receiving reports of the attack there. Marsh's column passed by houses in flames and met streams of refugees fleeing toward the fort. Several corpses were found scattered along the roadside.

When Marsh and his men reached Redwood Ferry, they were ambushed by a large war party after possibly being deceived by an Indian who told Marsh that there were no hostiles on the opposite bank of the river. By one account, when Marsh and his men eventually boarded the ferry they came under withering fire from places of concealment on both sides of the stream. Another widely credited version has the company cut off on three sides before boarding the ferry, immediately taking casualties. This account has Marsh leading his already decimated column into a thicket of trees and brush on the north side of the river. Moving through the foliage, they fought from that position well into the afternoon. Finally reaching the end of the tree-lined area, they could see the route back to the fort blocked by large numbers of Sioux. Marsh then decided to lead his men on a swim across the river. By reaching the opposite bank they could perhaps make it back to the fort. A short distance into the swim, Marsh was seized by a cramp and drowned. A young sergeant, John F. Bishop, then led 15 survivors, five of them wounded, safely back to the fort. In the hours that followed, eight more eventually trickled in.

Before the first day of the war was over Marsh and more than 20 of his men were dead. It would be two weeks before their bodies were recovered. Left at the fort that morning were 25 mostly untrained volunteers led by a baby-faced 19-year old lieutenant, Thomas P. Gere, who was ill at the time.

The Sioux's last minute decision not to attack the fort provided a desperately needed respite for Ridgely's defenders. In the interregnum, barricades were quickly constructed linking the main stone buildings into a more defensible compound. By late in the day on the 19th crucial reinforcements began flowing into the fort. One of the first and largest contingents was led by Lieutenant Timothy Sheehan, a handsome, dark-haired Irishman who came from Fort Ripley with 50 men from Company B of the 5th Minnesota Volunteer Infantry Regiment. A courier had found them in bivouac at Glencoe, 42 miles away. Sheehan left immediately, force-marching his men the entire distance, picking up young E.W. Earle, found wandering in the countryside, along the way. When Sheehan arrived at Fort Ridgely, he became the ranking officer on the installation and assumed overall command.

Another group of about 50 riflemen came from Renville County. Led by Lieutenant James Gorman and calling themselves the Renville Rangers, they were volunteers for the Union Army on their way to enlist at Fort Snelling. On the night of the 18th a courier from Fort Ridgely had caught up with them at St. Peter. Advised of the catastrophe unfolding in the Minnesota River Valley, they turned around and reached the fort by the following night. With their arrival and that of other assorted volunteers, mostly from St. Peter, by nightfall on the 19th, Sheehan had about 180 men under arms.

Three of them were Rieke brothers George, Victor, and Adam, who offered their services to Lieutenant Sheehan. Assigned to an artillery piece commanded by Dennis O'Shea, a local area resident, their job was to assist the gun crew by supplying a steady stream of shells for the weapon.

Another brother, Henry, was sick at the time—the nature of the illness is uncertain—and was at some point taken to the infirmary, which had been set up on the second floor of the stone barracks building.

Fifteen-year old sister Mary Rieke would play a significant role in the saga that followed. Assigned by Lieutenant Sheehan to the second floor of the barracks, she was asked to help look after the women, children, aged, and infirm who had taken refuge there and if possible to keep them away from the windows when the firing began. It is not known if Sheehan knew that Mary could speak the Sioux language. The defenders of Fort Ridgely were very fortunate that she did.

Also on the second floor of the barracks were a small group of Indian women, probably there as laundresses and cleaning ladies, who had been sent as spies by Little Crow to determine the strength of the fort. The women conversed freely in the Dakota tongue, not realizing that Mary could understand what they were saying. Mary overheard one of the women say that it would be a good time to attack. The woman then started to leave to inform Little Crow of the fort's limited strength. Mary called for help and ran after her, trying to stop the woman on the stairwell.

Mary later wrote, describing what came next:

> I was not strong enough to keep her back. She got out.
> Then I ran to find an officer and met Lt. Sheehan at the
> door. He immediately followed her. I picked up a piece of
> paper which the squaw had dropped and gave it to Shee-
> han as soon as he came back, from which he afterwards
> learned that she was a spy. When he brought her back he
> said "One moment more and she would have been gone."
> He brought her upstairs and left her in my care...

Ridgely was never intended as a war-fighting venue; it was not surrounded by a protective stockade. The fort's purpose was to provide administrative facilities, support treaty enforcement efforts, and house the units that patrolled the two agencies. Ridgely's most notable feature was a large open courtyard about 90 yards wide, centrally located and surrounded by a granite commissary building, barracks, and officer quarters. Associated utility buildings common to all military posts were scattered at varying distances outside the central compound.

Nor was the location particularly suited for defense. Deep ravines on three sides allowed intruders to venture unobserved to within shooting distance of the fort. The several utility buildings outside of the main courtyard provided cover for attackers. Lastly, incongruously, the fort had no internal water supply. Soldiers had to take a wagon to the foot of the bluff, a distance of about a mile, fill barrels from the spring-fed creek, and transport the load back to the fort—an impossible task if the post was under siege. Water was "stockpiled" by defenders, however August in Minnesota could be very warm and an extended siege would pose difficulties. A supply would also need to be held in reserve to fight fires and to quench the thirst of the garrison and the refugees who were streaming to Ridgely. Victor Rieke's perilous trek to the creek two days before had helped replenish the fort's supply and momentarily ease the otherwise dire circumstance confronting the fort's defenders.

Before the fighting began, John Buechro's wife asked him to return to their farm near Mud Lake and retrieve the family's prized possessions. Along with an army veteran friend, Buechro left that morning driving a wagon pulled by a team of oxen. He made it safely to his home, loaded the family's valuables, and with his companion began their return to the fort. Not far into their journey they were attacked by a party of Sioux. Both John and his friend and at least one Sioux brave were killed during the encounter that followed.

As refugees continued to stream in, those who were able and wished to partake were posted on the firing lines. Others were sheltered in the upper stories of the granite buildings.

Led by Sheehan, frantic efforts were made to prepare the fort for an attack that would surely come soon and in massive numbers. In work that went on around the clock, the barricades connecting the buildings around the central square were further strengthened and medical supplies, water, food, and ammunition were positioned at key points in the buildings and along the walls. Work was still going on when Sioux approached the fort on August 20. Posted in buildings and on the surrounding barricades, Sheehan's riflemen awaited the attack.

The assault came around midday, launched by 400 or more warriors using nearby ravines as cover. The Sioux's intention was to hit the fort simultaneously from all sides, with the main strikes coming from a ravine to the north and from across flat ground to the east. First, though, a small group led by Little Crow would sortie from the ravine that ran closest to the fort, acting as a diversion to draw attention away from other sections along the perimeter. Firing from the north would signal the launch of the all-out attack.

Sheehan responded to Little Crow's decoy by deploying 24 men in a line to the west. Placed in tall grass, they would be among the first to fire when the battle began in earnest. A second squad was positioned south of the fort, near a troublesome ravine that ran to within 300 feet of the fort's southeast corner. A third unit of 20 men was on its way to a point southwest of the second company when Little Crow sprang his trap.

Coordination was lacking, however, and the intended simultaneous assaults did not achieve the intended effect. Still, the fighting was intense all along the perimeter and Sheehan soon put his entire force on the barricades with orders to fire at will.

The first and ultimately one of the most dangerous attacks came from the ravine northeast of the fort. Dozens of attackers emerged from cover and raced toward the fort. Their attack carried to a row of exterior log buildings that paralleled the northeast wall. A group led by Lieutenant Gere immediately jumped from the barricades to meet them. At one point, warriors made it over the barricades and into the main compound before forces shifted from other points along the perimeter drove them back.

As would be the case at many threatened points throughout the battle, the fort's cannon proved to be decisive in repelling the intruders. The fort had six of them, a combination of 6-pound field guns, 12-pound howitzers of various types, and a large 24-pound howitzer. Fort Ridgely's artillery was under the overall command of Sergeant John Jones, a military "lifer" who had fought in the Mexican War. Thanks to his efforts, the post's ordnance was ably maintained, provisioned, and served by trained crews. (Because of a shortage of manpower, it is uncertain how many of the weapons could be operated at the same time.) Like many others at Ridgely that day, Jones soldiered on in the face of personal loss. As the battle was raging, his wife gave birth to a stillborn child.

In a pattern that would repeat itself through the long, difficult day, when Sioux warriors initially expelled from the central compound took possession of log buildings outside of the north wall, concentrated cannon fire drove them off. Two artillery pieces, one posted on the east corner of the compound, the other on the north, poured rounds of canister into the buildings. Coming from near point blank range, the withering fire broke up the attack, shattering buildings and setting many on fire. The Sioux fled, stunned by their first experience with the effects of the large weapons.

One of those who fought in the clashes near the log cabins was young E.W. Earle, who after his hair-raising experience had reached the fort along with others gathered up by the reconnaissance patrol. After first being posted as a rifleman in one of the buildings, he was later sent to positions on and outside the barricades. As fighting intensified, he stood up to take careful aim and was struck in the hand, damaging a finger and breaking a bone. Treated by the fort's surgeon, he later returned to action, confined for a time to lookout duties as he was unable to handle a weapon.

During the course of the long afternoon, attacks came at the fort from all quadrants. Soon after the log buildings had been cleared, a major assault was launched from the southwest. Attacking from a large ravine, the Sioux struck at the west corner of the compound, an area held by some of the Renville Rangers. Formed initially in a battle line to meet the attack, the Rangers fell back into the fort, taking casualties along the way. The Indians then surrounded the cluster of log cabins—married enlisted men's quarters—that were north of the stone barracks. Lieutenant Gere with Company B and additional Renville Rangers ran to meet the assault, which had almost carried to some frame buildings near the fort's northeast corner. Inside the fort, cannon crews fired the 12-pounder to help clear the road to the east and then shifted to aid Gere whose counterattack was pushing forward but losing men along the way.

When the massive attack began in the afternoon, the field gun served by the Rieke brothers was located in an exposed position on the southwest corner of the fort. The Riekes had manned that post since early on the previous day. Other than for a few sips of water they would not receive any sustenance until near sundown when after a day of fighting Lieutenant Sheehan brought each of them a few crackers. Almost immediately brought under fire at the outset, the weapon was pulled back into the parade grounds. The move left the gun and its crew several yards from the protection of the stone barracks on open ground vulnerable to incoming fire.

Adam Rieke later described the events that followed. He wrote that as the fight went on, someone was needed to take ammunition from the stone barracks to the gun crew—a position that was being raked with heavy fire. After first failing in his attempts to secure assistance for an action that the Riekes regarded as suicidal, Sergeant Jones rolled the shells on the ground toward the gun. The brothers, lying near the weapon in a position that allowed them to help shift it from place to place, then picked up the shells and handed them to the gunners.

The danger of the position was made obvious a few minutes later when a musket ball struck one of the gun crew, Private Andrew Rutledge, blowing away his jaw, tongue, and many of his teeth.

For the Riekes that tragedy was compounded. Watching from the window of the barracks infirmary was their younger brother Henry. Thinking that it was one of his brothers who had been struck, Henry fell into shock. Already frail from a serious illness, the effect was too much. He died four days later, likely from shock or a heart attack.

As other defenders raced to assist, the Indians continued to press their assault against the vulnerable corner. Sheehan's men answered with heavy rifle fire and shells from two of Jones' 12-pound howitzers. When the assault carried to the barricade, rifle fire from the Rangers and double canister loads from a 6-pound field gun decimated the attackers.

Thus the bloody day continued as strikes from the south and west soon followed. They were broken up by cannon fire that blew apart each attempt, inflicting heavy damage on attackers. Finally, at about six o'clock in the evening after five hours of almost constant combat, the Sioux broke off the attack, stunned by the ferocity of the defense and by artillery fire so intense that the sound could be heard miles away.

Still, the crisis was not over. It seemed quite obvious that the Sioux would return, perhaps in even greater strength. Though exhausted and emotionally drained, the fort's defenders and the refugees clustered inside began making preparations to meet the next attack. Barricades were repaired using grain sacks and cordwood and further extended between buildings. A barrier of cordwood four feet high and more than 100 feet long was built along the southwest corner of the fort. Supplies of drinking water were replenished. Shelters were constructed for artillery crews, enabling them to serve their weapons without exposure to gunfire. Bullets which had ricocheted off the fort's granite buildings were retrieved, molded and recast for use. The two howitzers were positioned in the middle of the compound. Handled by Sergeant Jones, the weapons were used to periodically lob shells into ravines and other Sioux gathering spots as much as a mile away to disrupt potential attacks. Finally, well aware of the ominous Sioux presence that continued to push against the fort from all directions, Sheehan sent a courier hurrying to St. Paul to update Governor Ramsey on conditions at the fort and urge him to send reinforcements at first opportunity.

FORT RIDGELY: AUGUST 22

MEANWHILE, reinforcements had also arrived at the Sioux camp. Four hundred braves from bands farther north bulked up Little Crow's force to perhaps as many as 1,200 fighters.

After having ranged unchecked across the landscape on August 18, the strength of the defenses at New Ulm and Fort Ridgely over the following two days had surprised the Sioux.

Taken aback after their assaults had been fiercely opposed, Little Crow and other Dakota leaders sought to restore the momentum by follow-up strikes against both locations. The newly arrived additional manpower would give them a decided numerical edge.

Prior to the second assault on Fort Ridgely, the Sioux made adjustments to their plan of attack. The overall concept still called for strikes from all sides. Once again ravines would be used to position war parties close to the barricades. This time, however, fire would be concentrated on the artillery crews. If the soldiers manning the weapons could be pinned down, that would enable assault parties to reach the barricades and overwhelm the defenders.

A second innovation was to make extensive use of fire arrows. Conflagrations would threaten defensive positions and divert manpower as the fort's defenders battled to control the flames.

On the morning of August 22, Sioux warriors exploded out of nearby ravines. Better coordinated this time, the 800 to 1,000 warriors hit the fort almost in unison. Taken under heavy fire almost immediately they ran toward the barricades, stopping momentarily in tall prairie grass to reload and seek cover.

They were confronted by a wall of rifle fire from all along the barricades. The fort's cannons were used to great effect, tearing apart clusters of warriors that massed together during the assault.

The initial attack, on which the Sioux had placed high hopes, was forced back. The attempt would be but the first of many as the Dakotas continued to hammer at the fort. At times during the struggle, groups of Sioux made it to the wooden utility buildings north of the main compound. Fort Ridgely's cannons, loaded with heated shot, were turned on the dwellings, shattering them with shell fire and burning them down. During the course of the battle, warriors reached the stables and other structures south of the main portion of the fort. Here too, artillery rounds set the buildings on fire and drove the attackers away.

George, Victor, and Adam Rieke were part of that action, serving the gun crew that engaged in the bitter fighting along the southwest side of the fortification. The ferocious attack penetrated the fort's outer defenses, reaching the sutler's store, which the Sioux overran and occupied. Using ammunition carried by the Riekes, Dennis O'Shea's cannon and a second field piece set fire to the building, killing the Sioux who had taken possession of it.

As the struggle intensified, heavy smoke engulfed the battlefield, making it difficult to see or breathe but providing temporary protection for the gun crews by obscuring them from view. An assault struck the barricades hastily erected the day before, carrying well into the perimeter defenses. As warriors began swarming over the ramparts, cannon fire again broke up the attack, forcing the Sioux to fall back to the shelter of a nearby ravine.

Though repelled time and time again, the Sioux assaults continued through the long day. Their lack of success extended to the embellishments the Sioux had added to the attack plan. Fire arrows had little effect. Recent rains had dampened building exteriors and the fires that started were quickly extinguished. The Sioux's attempt to hold the gun crews at risk had little impact. Smoke from scattered blazes and rifle and artillery fire was heavy, at times obscuring the crews. The inadvertent screen provided a degree of safety to the artillerymen while affecting marksmanship on both sides.

As the battle raged, the 24-pounder was used with good effect, impacting on groups at considerable distance from the perimeter. As some point in mid-battle Little Crow was knocked unconscious when a round from the large weapon struck close by.

When Little Crow was injured—he would be out of action for three days—other Sioux leaders decided to launch one final, all-out attack. This assault would be different. This time the entire Sioux force would be massed in one location and thrown against a single portion of the wall. The south-west ravine was chosen as the jumping off point.

It took considerable time to move hundreds of warriors and reposition them from different points on the battlefield. It was approaching evening before all arrangements were in order. Finally, they were ready.

When the attack came, it was massive in size. Sioux numbering in the hundreds sprang from the ravine and raced toward the southwest corner of the barricade.

They were met immediately with withering fire as rifles flashed from all along the barricade. Cannon shots from artillery pieces mounted at the south and west corners of the compound tore into the attackers. For the first time, canister rounds were fired from the 24-pounder. The effects were devastating. Despite their overwhelming advantage in numbers, the combined barrage was too much for the Sioux to overcome. As darkness came over the battlefield, they broke off the attack and returned to their village. A small contingent remained behind to observe activities and maintain a threatening presence.

The two battles had been difficult, closely fought affairs. Officially, the garrison had suffered 19 casualties—six killed and 13 wounded. The extent of Dakota losses is uncertain. An after action report estimated 100. That figure is speculative, however, as the Sioux—like most tribes—made consider-able efforts to carry away their dead and wounded.

Although it would not be certain for several days, the Sioux intended no further strikes on Fort Ridgely. Once again there was a degree of irony in that decision. The Sioux had in fact been confronted by a formidable defense during their two attempts and were stunned by the firepower that faced them. Unknown to them, the fort's defenders were essentially out of rifle ammunition and very few artillery rounds remained. So desperate was the garrison for rifle shells that during intervals in the fighting, women from the post collected spent bullets and remolded them during the battle using a ground floor room in the barracks to build cartridges. Led by Eliza Muller, the wife of the post surgeon — who also carried coffee to the defenders and helped care for the sick and wounded — by the narrowest of margins the women's efforts sustained the riflemen on the walls. Before the fighting was over, the situation became so acute that iron bars were cut into pieces that could fit down the barrel of a rifle The defenders were firing those when the battle ended and they had very little of the makeshift ammunition remaining.

Both battles at Fort Ridgely were waged with an intensity seldom matched by any of the wars fought on American soil against Native tribes. In his later years, George Rieke eloquently recalled the sound and fury of the desperate combat.

> *During both battles, and especially that of the second day, the pandemonium was indescribable. The roar of the cannon, the shriek of shell, crashing of solid shot, the shouted commands of the officers, the never ceasing, blood-curdling war-whoops of the Indians was enough to strike terror into the stoutest heart, yet those men, many of whom had never been under fire before, moved about with as much coolness and precision as they would have done had they only been firing a cannon at a Fourth of July celebration.*

NEW ULM: AUGUST 23

THE CITIZENS of New Ulm and the tens of dozens of others seeking refuge in the city could hear the sounds of battle coming from Fort Ridgely. The booming of the fort's cannon was clearly audible across the 20 mile distance. No one knew how the fight was going or what conditions the defenders were facing, however.

Since the first attack on the city, the townspeople had used the four day interregnum to further bolster the town's defenses. Conditions inside the city, though, were difficult in the extreme. Torrential downpours turned the city's streets into quagmires. The influx of refugees was beginning to stress the food supply. Sanitation became an increasing problem as immigrants were crammed into rooms where they remained 24 hours a day. One group of women and children took shelter in the brick basement of the Erd Building. Having seen the aftermath of the killings and rampant atrocities as they fled towards the city, they were resolved not to be taken alive by the Sioux. They placed a keg of gunpowder inside the room and were determined to take their own lives and, hopefully, some of the attackers, if the invaders reached the basement. At another haven for women and children at the Dakotah House, conditions became so congested that the women had to remove their hoop skirts to provide sufficient space to move around. At the Dakotah House, an area was also set aside as a makeshift hospital. One of the doctors who tended the sick and wounded there was William Mayo, who two decades later would establish the Mayo Clinic.

In a more positive vein, the city's defenders had received welcome reinforcements. The largest group, some 125 men from St. Peter and Le Sueur, increased the defenders strength to about 300 armed men. The company of Frontier Guards was led by Charles Flandrau. A lawyer by training, Flandrau, after earlier ventures as a merchant seaman, was at the time of the battle a justice in the Minnesota Supreme Court. Flandrau had no formal military training but by general consensus emerged as the leader of New Ulm's defense.

The day did not begin well for the town's defenders. At about eight o'clock in the morning, Flandrau was alerted to scouting reports of smoke across the river. Assuming the fires came from an approaching war party, he dispatched a mounted force of about 75 men to identify the threat and launch a spoiling attack on the oncoming warriors. As the militiamen moved toward the attackers, they were confronted by a force several times their own size. More significantly, their maneuvers enabled the Sioux to cut off their line of retreat back to the city. The militia company was forced to flee, riding far to the north to escape. Their race to safety took them out of the battle and stripped the city of a quarter of its riflemen.

An hour and a half later, at about nine-thirty, Dakota braves in immense numbers—probably 650 to 1,000 or more — approached the city. Led by chiefs Mankato and Big Eagle, they made no attempt at concealment. Their numbers stretched from horizon to horizon, surrounding the entire city.

Flandrau's intention was to deploy skirmishers in front of the barricades to halt, or at least delay, the attackers before they reached the city's inner defenses. Firing, yelling, sprinting down the bluff, hundreds of painted warriors came racing toward the city. Flandrau's skirmish lines quickly came apart as riflemen broke and ran, seeking shelter behind the barricades. Most made it, barely ahead of large numbers of Dakotas who swarmed towards them. After a few hectic minutes, Flandrau and his officers managed to restore order, stopping the militia's flight and securing the perimeter defenses. The barricades held against the onslaught, but it was a desperately close call.

As fighting grew in intensity, buildings outside the perimeter became the focus of action. Dakotas occupied several, using them as firing positions and as cover to shield the movements of attacking parties. The effect was a rarity in the annals of Indian warfare — the battle for New Ulm became a street fight. Defenders made repeated sorties to roust Sioux fighters from vantage points whose control placed the outcome of the struggle in jeopardy. In many of the buildings, the fighting raged room-to-room, hand-to-hand. As the day wore on and the situation grew ever more ominous, Flandrau's men set fire to several buildings, the flames from those fires merging with those from buildings already torched by the Sioux.

Flandrau's purpose in firing the buildings—to prevent the Sioux from using them and to create unobstructed zones of fire outside the perimeter—generally had the intended effect. Eventually, fires raged unchecked from buildings throughout the city. As more and more buildings went up in flames, Dakota warriors found it increasingly difficult to move across areas now made more visible to New Ulm's riflemen.

Fires set by both sides played significant roles in the battle. In late afternoon, the Sioux ignited an enormous blaze on grassland southeast of New Ulm. Taking advantage of prevailing winds that pushed the smoke and flames directly toward the city, warriors followed the firestorm, penetrating at one point as far as the blacksmith shop only a few feet from the southeast perimeter. Other nearby buildings were also occupied, providing unobstructed fields of fire into the center section of New Ulm and the heart of the city's defense.

With major defensive positions along the perimeter now exposed, the battle had reached a crisis point. Recognizing that the Indian's possession of the vantage points placed the town in mortal peril, Flandrau ordered a counterattack. Personally leading the charge, Flandrau took his men over the top of the barricades straight at the enemy. The intensity of the attack momentarily surprised the Sioux, but the fighting quickly became ferocious, some of the most bitter on a day already marked by savagery.

As with the combat earlier in the day, much of the fighting was close in, sometimes with each room, each building, having to be lethally wrested from aggressive and determined foes. Eventually, as darkness approached, the cohesion of Flandrau's group and the intensity of the assault drove the Dakotas from the area. Four members of Flandrau's party were killed in the struggle. After the Sioux departed, he ordered that the buildings outside the perimeter defenses—about 40 percent of the town's dwellings—be burned.

The Dakota's defeat along the barricades brought the attack to a close. Furiously chased for a time by New Ulm defenders to ensure their departure was permanent, the bulk of the Dakota contingent retreated from the area.

Though the brutal combat in the streets became the most notable feature of the Second Battle of New Ulm, a separate unusual occurrence also threatened to tip the scales of the struggle. In midafternoon, militiamen posted on lookout points around the compound reported that a sizable group of replacements was approaching the city and would soon reach the barricades on the southeast. When a squad of defenders went out to greet them and guide them in, they came under a hail of fire. Some were killed. The "reinforcements" turned out to be Dakota warriors clad in apparel taken from looted houses or dead settlers. Catastrophe was only narrowly averted.

The fighting at New Ulm, particularly in the streets and houses near the barricades, was savage in the extreme. Of the 29 defenders killed during the battle, 23 lost their lives outside the perimeter in those locations.

Darkness fell on a shattered city illuminated by fires that burned fiercely in and around the town. By one count, 190 of the city's 250 buildings were burned to the ground. Many more were uninhabitable, damaged beyond repair. Almost none went unscathed.

The Dakotas did not return in force to New Ulm. The following morning 100 or so showed up for a time to snipe and threaten the city's inhabitants at long distance, but by midday that contingent was gone. New Ulm, like Fort Ridgely, had survived by the closest of margins. The city's supply of rifle ammunition was nearly depleted as were its stockpiles of food and medical supplies. Disease threatened the hundreds who had been confined for days in cellars and barricaded rooms.

Confronted by drastic shortages of essential goods and materials, and with the city in ruins, Flandrau ordered the evacuation of New Ulm. Bodies of the six defenders killed in the first battle and the 29 killed in the second were buried where space allowed. That afternoon wagons with some supplies made it into the city shielded by 150 volunteers. The next day, the 24th, was spent making preparations for the mass exodus. On Monday, August 25th, one week after the uprising began, the population of New Ulm and the hundreds of refugees who had taken shelter in the city—altogether more than 2,000 people—left for Mankato guarded by an escort of 300 men.

Slowed by roads made nearly impassable by the recent heavy rains, the caravan of 150 wagons, most pulled by teams of oxen, struggled to cover the 30-mile distance. The journey was arduous but all eventually arrived without further incident.

A LULL BETWEEN THE STORMS

TWICE DEFEATED at both New Ulm and Fort Ridgely, Sioux leaders met to consider next moves in what had become a difficult war. The losses had a wider, more subtle effect that extended beyond the battlefield. From the outset there had been a sizable "peace party"—members of the Dakota population who, while not necessarily enamored with existing conditions, were opposed to the war. Indeed, one of the principal Sioux leaders, Chief Wabasha, refused to participate in the fighting. After New Ulm and Fort Ridgely, the position of the peace party advocates solidified and opinions of some previously non-committed tribesmen began to shift.

On August 25, two days after the second battle of New Ulm, Little Crow and other Dakota leaders decided to shift the bulk of their fighting forces about 30 miles north to a location that had once been the Upper Sioux Agency. Most of that move was completed by August 28. At their new site at Yellow Medicine, they prepared to resume the fighting.

Though the conflict had not gone as Little Crow intended, he and other chiefs continued to believe success was possible. The damage they had inflicted, particularly on August 18, had been near-catastrophic. Even though they had later been checked at New Ulm and Fort Ridgely, the shock of the initial devastation would, some thought, make the white population's recovery time long and arduous.

Little Crow and his followers believed they had leverage in another area as well. To this point in the fighting they had taken about 300 prisoners. Most were women and children from white and mixed-blood settler families. Depending on the course the war took, the captives might serve as valuable bargaining chips.

The prisoners, though, proved to be a flash point for disputes within the tribe. While they might indeed provide cover in negotiations and their presence might deter attacks on Dakota encampments, members of the peace party were increasingly concerned that the captives might be put to death in piques of anger as retribution if the trend in the fighting took a turn for the worse. The effect of that action, they believed, would surely doom the entire tribe. They began to work in a more concerted fashion to wrest control of the captives from Little Crow and his warriors.

HENRY H. SIBLEY

SOON AFTER the uprising began, Minnesota Governor Alexander Ramsey asked his predecessor, Henry H. Sibley, to serve as colonel in the state militia forces. It was not an appointment that Sibley requested or welcomed, believing others were more qualified. Sibley did in fact lack military experience, but he was conscientious, an effective handler of people and organizations and well known and respected throughout the new state. He also knew the Sioux very well, having lived among them and traded with them for many years. His appointment was generally accepted without controversy.

Fifty-one years old when he took command, Sibley was described by a contemporary as a robust, athletic individual who spoke French and understood the Sioux language. A long and successful political career had concluded in his being elected as the first governor of the state of Minnesota. He served in that position from 1858–1860.

After accepting his appointment as colonel in the state militia, Sibley waited for a time to gather supplies and reinforcements. His force initially consisted of 10 companies of the 6th Minnesota Volunteer Infantry Regiment, a unit that had never been under fire. Most of its 940 soldiers were raw recruits only recently mustered into service. For a brief time, Sibley could also draw on about 400 volunteer cavalrymen. The availability of those troops was limited, however. Most left for home, taking their horses with them when it came time to harvest that year's crops. Their departure left Sibley with an infantry-heavy fighting force, not ideal for opposing fast-moving Sioux raiders.

On August 26, he sent an advance party to Fort Ridgely to sustain the garrison until he and the remainder of his 1,400-man force arrived the next day.

Not for the last time would Sibley encounter criticism for being slow to respond. Most of those criticisms had little merit. At the outset, he was short of everything—horses, wagons, ammunition. Most important, as events would quickly show, his men, about to the placed in harm's way for the first time, were woefully lacking in training.

When Sibley and his men reached Fort Ridgely, they came upon a sobering sight. The fort had barely survived. Although there was rejoicing when the ranks of militia marched in, the scope of the destruction was obvious. Fresh graves provided stark evidence of the cost. A short distance away in New Ulm, the scene was one of total devastation. The town was almost entirely burned to the ground. Only in the next few days would a few forlorn stragglers begin trickling back into the city that had been abandoned after the battle on August 23.

Henry Sibley had indeed stepped into a major war.

He would fight it with ill-trained, ill-equipped militia forces soon to be further handicapped by a shortage of horses as volunteers returned home to attend the harvest. The few weapons that were initially available to them were mostly old and antiquated, the state's better weapons having been supplied to units sent to fight in the Civil War.

Sibley quickly launched into a training program for his inexperienced soldiers. A few days into it the regimen was interrupted by the need for forces to respond to a crisis. At ten o'clock in the morning on August 31, a detail party had departed from Fort Ridgely to bury bodies at nearby homesteads—at least 16 were quickly found—and gather information on Sioux movements. The following day several more, possibly as many as 54, including the remains of 20 soldiers—Captain Marsh's company—ambushed on the first day of the war, were discovered as the party temporarily divided to search both the north and south sides of the Minnesota River.

The search parties, totaling about 160 to 170 men, recombined that night and camped near a long, narrow ravine called Birch Coulee. The battle that developed there in the pre-dawn hours of the following morning would be Sibley's first test.

The Peace Pipe
A friendship gift to the Rieke family from a Dakota tribal elder, the
sacred pipe was carved from a quarry near Pipestone, Minnesota.

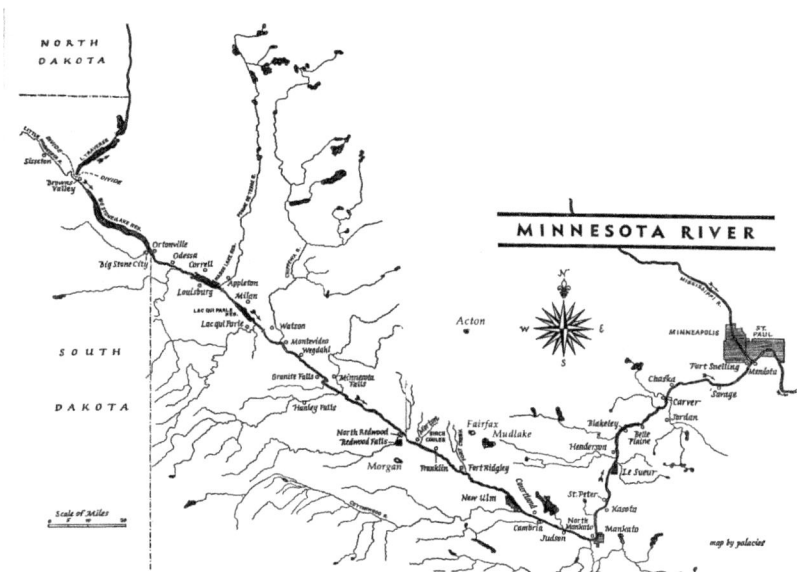

The Minnesota River

This portion of the young state of Minnesota was the focus of much of the action during the uprising. The Lower Sioux Agency was located near Redwood Falls. The Upper Sioux Agency was situated near the mouth of a stream below Granite Falls.

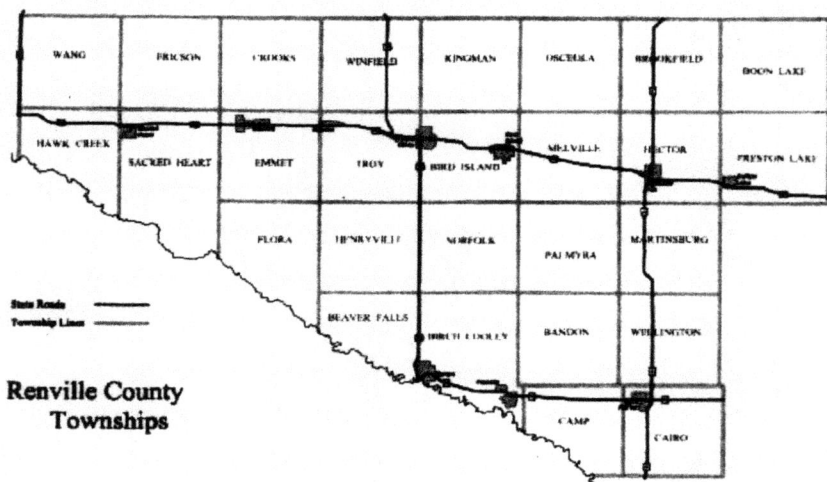

Renville County as organized at the time of the uprising. The Rieke and Buechro homesteads were in Cairo Township. Homes of the Earle, Wichman, and Henderson families were located in Beaver Falls. The Lammers and the Kietzmanns resided in Flora Township.

CAIRO TOWNSHIP

T. 112 N-R.32W
RENVILLE COUNTY, MINNESOTA

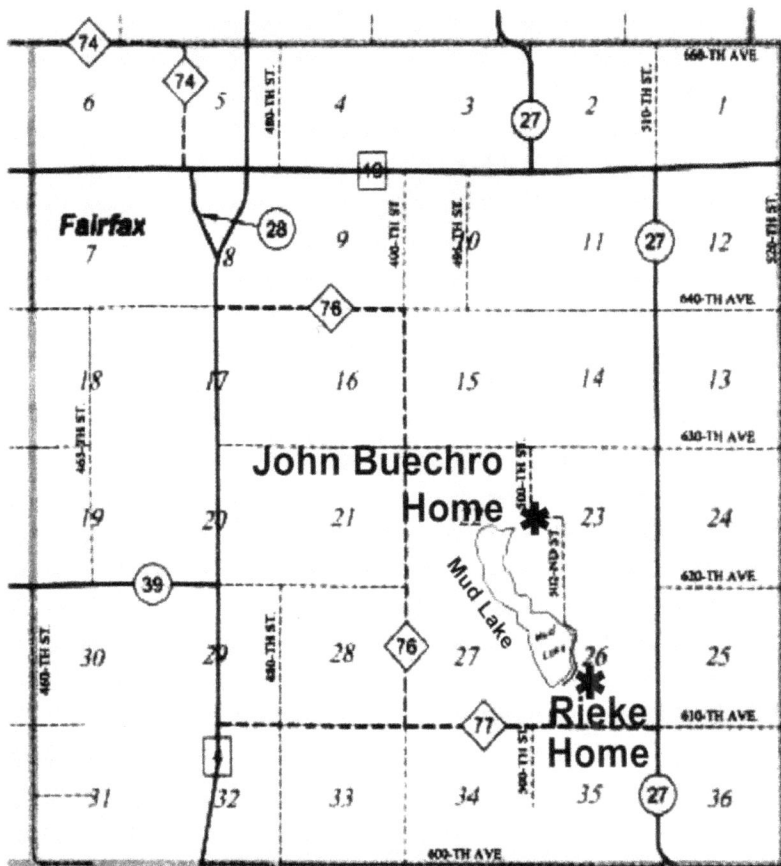

At the time of the uprising, the Buechro and Rieke homesteads were almost the only habitations in the sparsely settled township. Fort Ridgely is located about seven miles southwest of the Rieke home.

The George Rieke Family
George Rieke (seated second from left) and Sophie Lammers
Rieke (seated fourth from left) pictured with their children.
Circumstances brought George and Sophie together at Fort
Ridgely in the days following the uprising. Herman Rieke
(standing second from left) is the author's grandfather.

August Gluth Family
The family of August (seated, left) and Minnie (seated, right) in later
years. Annie (standing, second from left) married George and Sophie
Rieke's son Herman and became the author's grandmother.

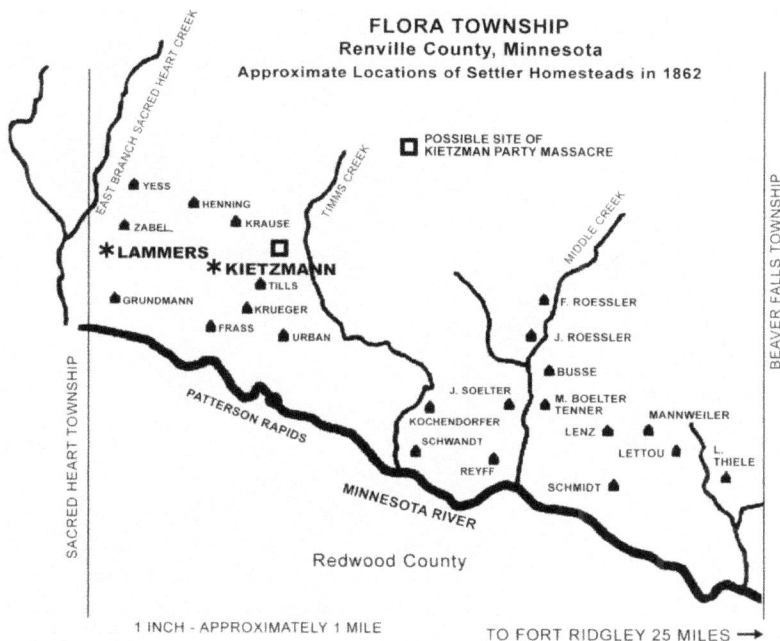

FLORA TOWNSHIP
Renville County, Minnesota
Approximate Locations of Settler Homesteads in 1862

POSSIBLE SITE OF
KIETZMAN PARTY MASSACRE

EAST BRANCH SACRED HEART CREEK

TIMMS CREEK

MIDDLE CREEK

BEAVER FALLS TOWNSHIP

YESS
HENNING
ZABEL
KRAUSE
*LAMMERS *KIETZMANN
TILLS
GRUNDMANN
KRUEGER
FRASS
URBAN

F. ROESSLER
J. ROESSLER
BUSSE
J. SOELTER
M. BOELTER
TENNER
KOCHENDORFER
SCHWANDT
LENZ
MANNWEILER
REYFF
LETTOU
L. THIELE
SCHMIDT

SACRED HEART TOWNSHIP

PATTERSON RAPIDS

MINNESOTA RIVER

Redwood County

1 INCH - APPROXIMATELY 1 MILE   TO FORT RIDGLEY 25 MILES ➝

*The Lammers and Kietzmann homesteads are in the northwest
portion of the township. The Kietzmann home was the gathering
point for the multi-family caravan that attempted to reach Fort
Ridgely on the first day. All except Sophie Lammers, her two
children, August Gluth and another teenager were killed.*

Little Crow
*The most influential of the Dakota leaders, though apparently not
initially disposed toward war, Little Crow became an implacable foe
and personally led many of the killing raids.*

John Other Day
*A full-blooded Sioux, Other Day saved the lives of more
than 60 settlers and led them on a three-day journey to
safety. He later scouted for the army.*

BEAVER FALLS TOWNSHIP
Renville County, Minnesota
Approximate Locations of Settler Homesteads in 1862

SMITH CREEK

BJORKMAN

IENENFELDT

SIEG

MEYER

HAUFF   ZITZLAFF

BEAVER CREEK

SHEPHARD

AHRENS   WICHMANN

WHITE
WEDGE   HENDERSON

✳ EARLE

D. CARROTHERS

J. CARROTHERS

HUNTER

DOYLE

ROBERTSON   JUNI

HAYDEN   BAHLKE
FROHRIP

EISENREICH

FLORA TOWNSHIP

BIRCH COOLIE TOWNSHIP

REDWOOD RIVER

MINNESOTA RIVER

REDWOOD COUNTY

TO FORT RIDGLEY ~ 15 MILES ⟶

1 INCH = APPROXIMATELY 1 MILE

Source: Mary P. McConnell - 2013

*E.W. Earle's home was located in the eastern portion of the township near
the neighboring Henderson and Wichman homesteads. Wichman was one of
the first to spread the alarm on August 18. Henderson was wounded during
an attempt to negotiate with a Sioux war party. His wife and two daughters
were slain on the first day of the uprising and Henderson was later killed at
Birch Coulee. Earle's mother was taken prisoner and his brother was killed
as the family attempted to flee to Fort Ridgely.*

E.W. Earle
*A teenager at the time, Earle narrowly escaped capture or death on
the first day of the uprising. He was wounded in the fighting at Fort
Ridgely and later fought at Birch Coulee.*

Louis Thiele
The Louis Thiele family in later years. (Louis is seated at right; his
third wife, Fredericke is at left.) Thiele's wife Elizabeth and four-
year old son were killed on the first day of the uprising. Thiele made
it to Fort Ridgely, participated in the post's defense and helped bury
the fatalities found scattered throughout the area. He later joined the
Union army and saw extensive service in the Civil War.

Lieutenant Thomas Gere
After Fort Ridgely's senior
officer was killed in the first
day of fighting, the 19-year old
lieutenant led the fort's defense
until additional forces arrived.

Charles E. Flandrau
*A justice in the Minnesota Supreme Court, Flandrau led a
company of Frontier Guards to New Ulm and emerged by
consensus as the leader of the city's defense.*

Fort Ridgely, 1862
Schematic of Fort Ridgely at the time of the uprising. The fort's purpose was to provide administrative facilities and billeting accommodations for the troops that patrolled the two Sioux agencies. It was not designed for defense.

Lieutenant Timothy Sheehan
Sheehan brought Company B of the 5th Minnesota Volunteer Infantry on a 42-mile forced march to Fort Ridgely, then assumed overall command of the fort. Later in the war he fought at Birch Coulee and in other encounters.

Sergeant John Jones
*A veteran artilleryman, Jones' adroit handling of Fort
Ridgely's ordnance played a vital role in the fort's successful
defense. He was later commissioned as an officer and
participated in the campaigns in Dakota Territory.*

Victor Rieke
Victor Rieke and his wife Mina pictured in about 1892. Prior to the first attack on Fort Ridgely, Victor drove a wagon to a nearby creek to replenish the fort's water supply. After filling several barrels, he made it back to the post as bullets and arrows whizzed past him.

Adam Rieke

*Adam Rieke, his wife Ernestine, and his daughter Anna,
circa 1890. Adam, along with his brothers George and
Victor, fought in the defense of Fort Ridgely.*

Mary Rieke and Charles Fenske
Mary Rieke pictured in later years with her husband. Fifteen years old at the time of the uprising, Mary's fluency in the Dakota tongue helped foil a plot to reveal information on Fort Ridgely's defenses.

Alexander Ramsey
As Governor of Minnesota through the initial phase of the war, Ramsey appointed his predecessor, Henry Sibley, to command the state's military units.

Henry Sibley
Appointed at the outset of the uprising to lead Minnesota's
militia forces, Sibley's eventual victory at Wood Lake brought
major fighting in Minnesota to a close. He later led successful
expeditions against the Sioux in Dakota Territory.

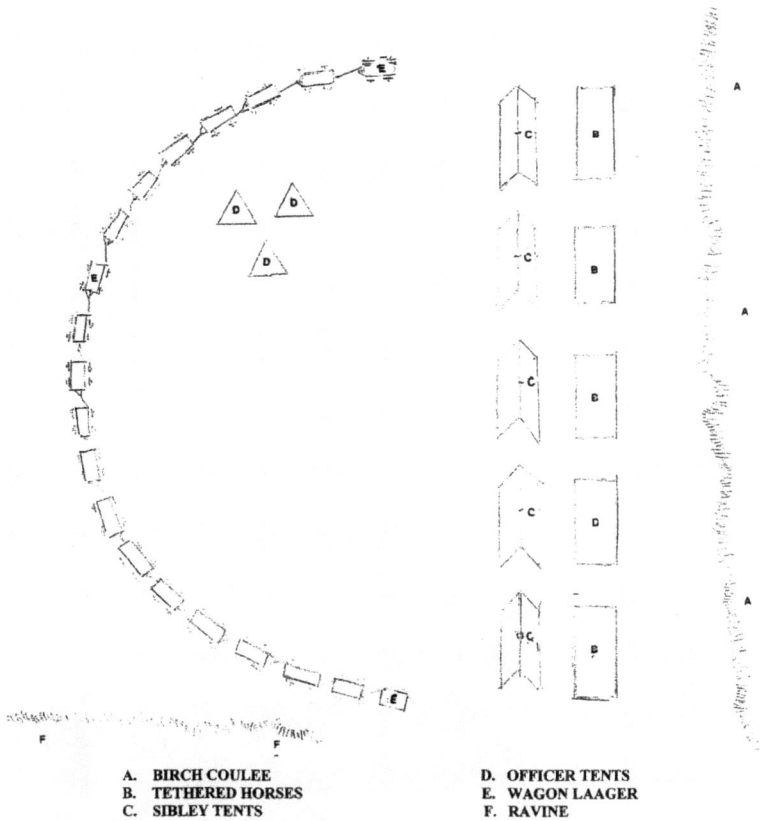

A. BIRCH COULEE	D. OFFICER TENTS
B. TETHERED HORSES	E. WAGON LAAGER
C. SIBLEY TENTS	F. RAVINE

Birch Coulee Battlefield

Vulnerable from all sides, the bivouac at Birch Coulee was ill-chosen. The site was placed under siege for two days by Sioux warriors who exacted a fearful toll on the defenders. The outcome of the battle re-energized the Sioux, who continued heavy raids throughout the region.

John Pope
Best remembered in history as the losing commander at
Second Bull Run, in his later service as commander of the
Department of the Northwest, Pope was perhaps the best
of the Union's departmental commanders.

Alfred Sully
Experienced in Indian warfare, Sully led major campaigns
in 1863 and 1864, winning major battles at Whitestone Hill,
Killdeer Mountain, and the Battle of the Badlands. His
exceptional tactics at Killdeer Mountain led to victory in
perhaps the largest battle of the Indian wars.

George and Sophie Rieke
In his later years, George Rieke began writing poetry and became a much-admired pillar of the Fairfax, Minnesota, community.

Fort Ridgely Monument
The massive pillar on the grounds of Fort Ridgely
memorializes the heroic defense of the fort. Among the names
inscribed on the monument are the brothers George, Victor,
and Adam Rieke and their sister Mary. The monument is
located on the spot where the fort's flagpole stood.

BIRCH COULEE: SEPTEMBER 2–3

THE CAMPSITE selected by patrol commander Major Joseph Brown (some scholars suggest that Brown was only nominally in charge and that the operational commander at Birch Coulee was in fact Captain Hiram P. Grant) was poorly suited for defense. Located near the remnants of the Lower Sioux Agency, the place was easily approachable under cover. Shielded by a deep ravine (Birch Coulee) to the east, a knoll to the west, tall grass to the north and a draw to the south, the camp was vulnerable from all sides. Attacks would indeed come from all directions, although as the fighting developed the heaviest would be struck from the north and south. The defenders wagons were configured in a semi-circle with soldiers bivouacked in 20-man tents placed inside the wagon park. Horses were tethered to wagons across the open arc of the circle nearest the ravine.

Well before dawn on September 2, perhaps as many as 200 Sioux out of a total contingent of around 350, their movements masked by the favorable terrain, began infiltrating the position. Using bows and arrows to silence their attack, they attempted to kill the sentries without awakening the sleeping troops. Possibly alerted by the nervousness of the horse herd, a picket sounded the alarm. The attack quickly drove in the camp's 10 sentries, killing one, as they ran for cover ahead of Dakota braves racing toward them out of the darkness. Inside the tents soldiers scrambled for safety as the Sioux unleashed breast-high volleys that shredded the canvas and wounded or killed several as they attempted to stand.

One of the soldiers inside the tents was young E.W. Earle. Though his hand was still heavily bandaged from the wound he had sustained at Fort Ridgely, he had attached himself to Major Brown's company as it was on its way to Birch Coulee. Asleep when the shooting began, he avoided injury by rolling out of the tent. Those who stood upright near him were struck by incoming fire.

Thirty soldiers were wounded or killed in the first few minutes. Survivors first attempted an ineffectual skirmish line, and then sought shelter in hastily dug rifle pits—the column had carried only four shovels with them—or behind overturned wagons and the carcasses of the company's horses, almost all of which had been killed in the early moments of battle, shot as they stood whinnying and exposed in the open. Desperate to escape the withering fire that seemed to come at them from all sides, militiamen dug entrenchments using whatever was available—drinking cups, mess gear, knives, bayonets—to carve shallow havens from the inferno surrounding them. E.W. Earle used a bayonet and his own hands to scoop out a small pit. Standing up or moving from place to place risked wounding or death.

With the soldiers pinned down and taking casualties, the Sioux chose to engage the defenders at long range, effectively placing the camp under siege. All through the long, hot day the soldiers remained pinned in place, most without food or water, their thirst made more severe by having to bite powder cartridges to prepare their weapons to fire. Wounded men begged for assistance to no avail. An indication, one of many, of how unprepared Brown's men were for combat was that when ammunition began to run low, they were resupplied with bullets of a caliber too large for their weapons. Soldiers used pocket knives, kitchen ware, and bayonets to shave down the shells enough to permit their use.

Reports of the battle carried to Fort Ridgely, 16 miles distant, where Sibley immediately sent out a 240-man rescue party led by Colonel Samuel McPhail. As McPhail's force, consisting of companies B, D, and E of the 6th Minnesota, a group of 50 mounted rangers, and a section of artillery, approached the Birch Coulee battlefield, McPhail was duped by a small party of Indians into thinking he was surrounded by a larger force. McPhail stopped, fell back two miles, set up a defense, and sent Lieutenant Sheehan for help. Chased by Dakota warriors almost the entire way, Sheehan made it to Fort Ridgely although his horse soon died from several wounds.

Sibley responded quickly with his entire remaining force—six companies of the 6th Minnesota and two recently arrived companies of the 7th Minnesota—reaching McPhail's position near midnight. At dawn he moved on, shelling the area in front of him as he progressed. Near Birch Coulee concentrated artillery fire scattered the Sioux, lifting the siege. Sibley rode into the battle site at midday of September 3. He found utter chaos. The soldiers at Birch Coulee had been under siege for the better part of two days. Some had gone without food or water the entire time. Thirteen soldiers were dead and 47 were severely wounded—four would die in the days that followed—and several others had sustained minor wounds. Among those killed at Birch Coulee was Mr. Henderson, E.W. Earle's neighbor, who had seen his wife and two young daughters murdered on the first day of the war. The carcasses of 87 horses littered the encampment.

More casualties were sustained at Birch Coulee than during any battle of the war. Sibley drew a lesson from the conduct of the battle and its outcome: His forces had to be more adequately trained. He returned to Fort Ridgely to begin doing that, determined if possible to delay putting his men into combat until they learned how to fight.

A WIDENING CONFLICT: THE BLOODY AFTERMATH OF BIRCH COULEE

ALTHOUGH THE FIGHT at Birch Coulee had ended with the Sioux being driven from the battlefield, the outcome was clearly a tactical victory for the tribesmen. Rejuvenated by the outcome, they continued heavy raids, striking at settlements throughout a wide region. Hamlets, some as far east as the present-day suburbs of Minneapolis, were terrorized by raiders who swept through settlements without warning.

Travel across the countryside even by sizable, well-armed groups, remained hazardous. On September 3 on the road between Acton and Hutchinson an army patrol was attacked by a large war party. The soldiers, about 55 new recruits of Company B, 10th Minnesota Volunteer Infantry, were riding in company wagons after breaking camp at sunup. Led by Captain Richard Strout, the soldiers fought a desperate, running battle. Six were killed and at least 15 were wounded before the company reached safety.

The following day settlements at Hutchinson and Forest City were attacked. Both towns had constructed stockades and other improvised fortifications. At Forest City a ten-foot-high palisade was built in a day. The town's citizens and refugees from nearby farms—estimated at about 250 in number—used logs that by a stroke of fortune had already been cut for planned construction. Though under siege for more than a week, they repelled attacks that came at them in varying sizes and intensities. While the defenses at Forest City and Hutchinson were sufficient to save the towns, buildings outside the perimeter at both locations were looted and burned. As attacks and pillaging continued over a widespread area, hastily constructed fortifications like those at Forest City and Hutchinson were thrown together at several settlements.

Meanwhile, travel and transportation in the area came to a stop. Traffic on the Red River was halted. Military couriers, mail carriers, and stage coach drivers were killed trying to reach Pembina, North Dakota, St. Cloud, Minnesota, and Fort Snelling.

Within a few days, fighting spread far to the north. Dakota warriors began attacking unfortified stage coach stops and river crossings on routes between Fort Garry (now Winnipeg, Manitoba) and St. Paul. Settlers and employees of the Hudson Bay Company took refuge in Fort Abercrombie, a tiny three-building outpost on the west bank of the Red River about 25 miles south of present-day Fargo, North Dakota. Built to guard steamboat traffic on the Red River and wagon trains on the way to Montana goldfields, the fort was attacked on August 30, September 3, and, most heavily, on September 6. At the outset, the small garrison consisted of 78 soldiers from Company B of the Fifth Minnesota led by Captain John Vander Horck. As at Fort Ridgely, artillery fire—the small post had three 12-pound mountain howitzers—would play a decisive role in fending off Sioux attacks.

Initially devoid of a stockade and lacking blockhouses, the fort's defenders faced another shortcoming as well. Earlier in the year it was discovered that the post's stocks of ammunition were mostly the wrong size—the shells did not fit the company's .69 caliber muskets.

News of the Sioux uprising in the east had reached Abercrombie by August 23. Conditions at the fort remained quiet until August 30 when a band of Dakotas drove off much of the garrison's grazing stock, which had been left unattended on the prairie about a mile from the fort. The next morning, Vander Horck dispatched a party that recovered about 50 head of cattle.

On September 3, 100 or so Sioux attacked the fort, striking at stables on the south edge of the installation in an attempt to ride off with army mounts and the horses of the civilians who had taken shelter at the fort. After about two hours, the defender' rifle fire and shells from the fort's howitzers drove the raiders away. Although sporadic fire from Indians hidden in the brush along the river continued for several hours, no further attacks were made against the fort. Two of the post's defenders were wounded, one of whom later died. Two Dakotas were found dead near the stable area. Four others may also have been killed and as many as 15 wounded.

The Sioux's heaviest and most threatening strike came at daybreak on September 6. The attack once again began with an attempt to take the stables. The effort succeeded momentarily as a group of warriors managed to reach and enter the buildings. After a few minutes of intense fighting, they were dislodged by soldiers and armed civilians who rushed to the scene.

The Sioux then shifted their attack, assailing the fort from all sides. Fighting continued for several hours and was particularly heavy around the fort's commissary building. Finally, the attackers withdrew, again taking cover along the riverbank from where they maintained sporadic fire. Two of the fort's defenders were killed and another wounded during the long day of action. Indian losses were believed to be so heavy that they gave up further attempts to overrun the fort. For the next several days they resorted to long-range sniping, often aimed at soldiers carrying water from the river. Like Fort Ridgely, Fort Abercrombie did not have a well or other internal water supply on the premises.

The small garrison survived under quasi-siege conditions until September 23 when a mixed force of 450 men from Fort Snelling and other locations fought its way into the post. Although skirmishes continued for another six days, the fort's survival was secured. With relief finally at hand, the civilian refugees who had taken shelter at the fort were moved to St. Cloud. Five soldiers were killed and five wounded during the multiple assaults that at times threatened to overrun the outpost. Indian losses — inflicted by soldiers, settlers, and artillery fire — were later described by Native sources as being unusually heavy.

The assault on Fort Abercrombie was yet a further indication that the outbreak, seeming at the outset to be confined to a portion of south central Minnesota, was in fact becoming a much wider conflict. At Sioux Falls, in present day South

Dakota, the Dakotas burned and looted much of the city after it had been abandoned by panicked townspeople who fled to Fort Yankton. In northwest Iowa, northeast Nebraska Territory, and a considerable portion of Wisconsin, farms and settlements were abandoned, creating streams of refugees seeking safety from the terror that seemed to be spreading all around them.

In Iowa, indicative of the expanding scope of the conflict and the terror that it evoked, the state hastily constructed a string of forts from Sioux City to Iowa Lake. Still haunted by memories of the 1857 Spirit Lake Massacre, in which settlers were killed and women taken prisoner, a law was quickly enacted authorizing the enlistment of 500 mounted men from the frontier counties. Though later rescinded, its hurried passage was a barometer of the prevailing climate of fear. While no fighting occurred in Iowa, the terror induced by the war led to the expulsion of most of the few remaining Natives left in the state.

THE NATIONAL GOVERNMENT RESPONDS

THE EXPANDING WAR had ripple effects far beyond the settlements in the states of Minnesota, Wisconsin, and Iowa and in Nebraska and Dakota territories. Nearly a third of the land area of the Union was proverbially, and in some cases literally, on fire. Food production for the civilian population in the east and for federal armies in the field was inhibited. Transportation slowed or ground to a halt in the war zone. Roads across a vast landscape were unsafe. With the flow of traffic in a condition of near-paralysis, business activity, mail delivery, and other interchanges of official and unofficial commerce slowed markedly.

The growing conflagration was affecting military recruiting in support of the national war effort. The region's state and territorial governors pleaded for help in putting down an insurgency that threatened to overwhelm the capabilities of local forces.

Their appeals for assistance came at an inopportune time. At this point in the war, the Union Army of the Potomac had not yet won a single major victory in the Eastern Theater. There was already a seemingly bottomless demand for troops to sustain a war that had witnessed armies, battles, and casualties of sizes not remotely foreseen at the outset.

The government, though, could not be perceived as being unable or unwilling to safeguard a significant segment of its population. Clearly, the negative implications of the uprising on the frontier were far too ominous to be left unaddressed. The national government was compelled to respond, and rapidly. The best case outcome would be to quickly put down the uprising or force the hostile bands farther west, away from the fields and population centers under threat.

The initial response of federal authorities was organizational and administrative in nature. On September 6, a new organization—the Department of the Northwest, with headquarters in St. Paul, was created to focus specifically on the threat in the region. The department was enormous in size, consisting of the states of Wisconsin, Minnesota, Iowa, and territories that now compose the states of North and South Dakota. On October 11, Nebraska Territory was added to the structure. (Montana Territory would be later appended on May 26, 1864.)

On September 16, President Lincoln appointed Major General John Pope to command the new department.

JOHN POPE

JOHN POPE is mostly remembered in American military history as the losing general at the Second Battle of Bull Run. The decisiveness of the defeat cost him command of his army. On taking command, Pope had boasted loudly of his earlier triumphs and ambitious intentions. While his words may have been intended to inspire his troops, they succeeded mainly in alienating soldiers already embittered by his having replaced Major General George McClellan, their popular favorite. As a result, he was regarded by his army and by much of the public as being a windy braggart. At times he was openly jeered by his troops who regarded his comments as a slur on their abilities and an indictment of their previous commander. There is truth, or at least a measure of truth, in many criticisms of Pope. At times and in varying degrees he was arrogant, verbose, and boastful. He was also at times and in varying degrees, opinionated, loudly profane, and a man of volcanic temper. But, as his later service would show, in the American West he was also one of the very best of the senior officers sent to wage war along America's frontier.

After his humiliating defeat at Second Bull Run, Pope's new assignment as commander of the Department of the

Northwest was regarded by many as a form of banishment. In the Northwest, though, Pope would write a second chapter to his story. He would prove to be an aggressive leader, a capable planner of major expeditions, an adroit handler of civil affairs, and perhaps the most capable of any of the Union's departmental commanders.

On September 16, Pope arrived in Minnesota and took official command. His exceptional energy and aggressiveness became immediately apparent.

He faced a daunting task. There was at first no staff or structure to assist him and no functioning quartermaster organization to buy mules and requisition materials and supplies. The only experienced troops in the entire department were the 3rd Minnesota Volunteer Infantry Regiment and a small portion of the 10th Minnesota. Colonel Henry Sibley, one of his major component commanders, was desperately short of horses. Wagons were also scarce although there was an immediately identified need for 500 or more.

Despite the formidable challenges, Pope pitched in with characteristic vigor, one of his first steps being to order 2,500 horses. He eventually received about 2,000, using them to convert his veteran units to mounted infantry and organize a regiment of rangers. By January 1863, Sibley would have 1,046 cavalrymen under his command. To strengthen his thinly manned garrisons, Pope found additional forces—first among them four regiments from Wisconsin—and quickly pulled them into the region. Unwilling to remain on the defensive, he advised Sibley to continue with his plans to go after the Sioux, telling him that he (Pope) would push forward everything he could to assist him as soon as men and supplies became available. With Sibley's initial concept as a basis, Pope moved ahead, establishing and garrisoning a chain of posts across the frontier. At a time when there was not a single soldier or military post in the hundreds of miles from Fort Randall to Fort Benton, Montana, in February 1863, Pope began planning a campaign aimed at ending terror attacks and driving the hostiles from Minnesota.

THE CAPTIVES

HAVING BEEN SAVED from death when a weapon misfired, Sophie Lammers and her two small children were forced to accompany Little Crow and the war party that had killed her husband and almost all other members of the settler caravan. Eventually she was placed in a camp with nearly 300 other captives, mostly women and children.

Sophie's experience in captivity was perilous in the extreme. Little Crow sometimes returned to camp at night in a drunken state having looted whiskey supplies left behind in abandoned homes and villages. On occasion, he would look for Sophie. However, Indian women accompanying the warriors would hide her—under buffalo robes according to the most often cited family story—until Little Crow fell asleep.

In one horrific incident, the chief asked Sophie to fetch water from a nearby stream. While she was away, he picked up her one and a half year old son and threw him in the camp fire. At great risk to himself, his six-year old brother raced to the fire and pulled the infant free. Remarkably, though in great pain and with no medicine except grease to put on the burns, the child survived.

Meanwhile, August Gluth, the 12-year-old whose life was spared because he could handle oxen and care for Little

Crow's ponies, traveled with the Sioux party for six weeks, an eye-witness to torture and to numerous killings of white settlers.

Soon after his capture, he made the first of his escape attempts. Quickly recaptured, he was threatened with death by Little Crow if he attempted to break free again. During his forthcoming days as a prisoner, August, who already knew some Sioux words, became fluent in the language. Using that facility to gauge when the moment was right, he broke away a second time. He got farther on that try but again was caught and taken forcibly back to Little Crow's camp. Immediately on his return a Sioux warrior took out his tomahawk and swung at August's head. The boy ducked away, receiving a glancing blow that left a sizable gash and covered his face in blood. As the warrior prepared to hit him a second time, Little Crow happened upon the scene and stopped the attack, saving August's life. The motive is not entirely clear but likely had to do with Gluth's solicitous care in tending to Little Crow's ponies. The wound eventually healed and August continued his duty as primary groom for the chief's horses.

Still, horrified by conditions in the camp and by the wanton killings he had observed, Gluth remained determined to escape. After about six weeks in captivity, he saw an opportunity and slipped away from camp. Having learned from his previous tries, he was now more adept at conceal-ment. Hiding in clumps of bulrushes and reeds along the sloughs, he subsisted mainly on wild berries and crawfish, which he peeled and ate raw.

Staying barely ahead of his pursuers, Gluth edged closer to Fort Ridgely and safety. After a time, he came within sight of the fort only to be seen by two warriors who had been tracking him. August jumped from his hiding place amid some bulrushes and made a dash for safety. Chased by the braves and about to be overtaken, August's plight was seen by a small mounted patrol who hurried to his rescue. The patrol took him to Fort Ridgely where he remained until bloodshed in the nearby area ended.

Although their success at Birch Coulee had reenergized the pro-war faction among the Dakotas, there continued to be disquiet among the considerable segments of the population who had from the outset been less than enthusiastic or outright opposed to the war. For many, their misgivings increased as it became evident that additional soldiers in large numbers were moving into the area. Even before reinforcements came, the settlers' resistance had been surprisingly fierce. Far from breaking after being subjected to abject horror on August 18 and the days after, as had been the Dakotas' hope, the Minnesotans had thus far withstood the cataclysm.

Though Little Crow's group still held sway in the tribe, here and there groups broke away—some to fight in smaller, more mobile bands, some to avoid conflict altogether, others to venture west to get out of immediate danger and await future events. Sizable numbers went to Canada.

In the midst of the tribe's internal turbulence, the situation concerning the nearly 300 captives grew increasingly uncertain. There was growing fear among members of the peace party that the captives might be harmed in reprisal by Little Crow and his followers if the conflict took a turn for the worse.

Physical control of the captives and decisions about what to do with them became contentious issues within the tribe. Even within the war faction, treatment of captives was unpredictable. While the majority were ill-used—many were physically abused, stripped of most of their clothing and nearly starved—a few received solicitous care from their captives. Mary Schwandt, taken with three other women (one of whom later died) when the wagon they were in was captured on August 18, credited a friendly Dakota woman with safeguarding her. The two other women taken with her were not as fortunate—they were repeatedly assaulted by their captors. Mrs. Harriet Adams, whose six-month old child died after being held by the feet and repeatedly flung against the wheels of a wagon, was protected by a warrior who treated her like a sibling. Little Crow himself is said to have watched out for Mrs. Joseph Brown (a Dakota woman married to a white man) and her children after she bravely confronted her Sioux captors.

Treatment sometimes varied even within the Sioux family groups with whom the prisoners were incarcerated. Seven-year old Minnie Buce was held for a time with a Dakota family that consisted of an adult male, an older wife with a teenage son, and a young wife with an eight-year old boy. Minnie was well cared for by the adult male (ironically, he was the Dakota warrior who had killed her parents) and the young wife and her son. As opportunities presented, she was subjected to abuse by the older wife and the teenage son.

As the conflict continued, some peace party members went so far as to help small numbers of captives escape. Others attempted to communicate with Colonel Sibley, seeking to leverage their own position in a favorable way in return for a promise to assure safe return of the prisoners.

Sibley was not yet in a position to negotiate, however, and Little Crow and his followers believed another major victory would turn the war in their favor.

A few days later, at Wood Lake, they would seek that decisive triumph.

WOOD LAKE: SEPTEMBER 23

AFTER BRINGING HIS main force to Fort Ridgely on August 28, Henry Sibley had remained there, drilling his troops on a daily basis. The encounter at Birch Coulee had interrupted his training regimen while at the same time demonstrating how desperately it was needed. In the immediate aftermath of the battle, training was resumed and intensified. Finally, initial installments of badly needed supplies began reaching the fort. On September 11, a consignment of 50,000 rounds of ammunition arrived. September 13 and 14 saw the delivery of clothing and other materiel. September 13 also brought the first influx of experienced troops when 270 soldiers from the 3rd Minnesota Volunteer Infantry Regiment, veterans of Civil War action, reached the fort.

As his forces increased in strength and capability Henry Sibley, though desperately short of mounted troops—the loss of 90 horses at Birch Coulee and the departure for home of much of his volunteer cavalry had stripped him of almost all of his horsemen—set out to engage the Dakotas. On September 19, he left Fort Ridgely with more than 1,500 men. With the newly arrived 3rd Minnesota, nine companies of the 6th Minnesota, five companies of the 7th Minnesota, a contingent of Renville Rangers, portions of the Fifth and 6th

Iowa State Militia, assorted civilian militia, and civilian artillerymen crewing a six-pound cannon, Sibley moved generally
northwest, heading for a location about 40 miles away near
the Upper Sioux Agency where Sioux in large numbers were
believed to be gathering.

On the evening of September 22, Sibley encamped on a
roughly triangular perimeter formed by ravines and the east
shore of Lone Tree Lake, about five miles north of present-
day Echo, Minnesota. (The forthcoming fight, known as the
Battle of Wood Lake, is somewhat misnamed. Wood Lake is,
in fact, about three and a half miles west of the site of the
encounter.) Sibley positioned the 6th Minnesota on the lake
front on the left side of his bivouac. To that unit's immediate
right the 3rd Minnesota camped on the crest of a ravine. The
7th Minnesota held ground to the right rear of the ravine,
forming a three-sided defensive alignment.

During the night, Little Crow led 700 to 1,000 warriors to
the bivouac area and positioned them in tall grass near the
camp. Little Crow's plan was well conceived, anticipating
that when Sibley broke camp the next morning the soldiers
would move slowly with most riding in wagons formed in
column, the chief envisioned an ambush followed by an
attack from all sides. The trap was laid on the road leading
from the campsite about a half mile from the bivouac. After
allowing the lead column to pass, warriors would strike the
supply wagons that followed, isolating Sibley's artillery and
rendering it less effective.

When the ambush was underway, a second group of Dakotas would launch a heavy attack from a ravine that ran near
the road not far from Sibley's right flank. A third group

would strike from the left while a fourth smaller cadre would go straight for Sibley and his headquarters element.

Little Crow's plans to attack as Sibley's men were breaking camp was foiled when a group of soldiers rose early to venture out to look for food to supplement their rations. Traveling in wagons, they moved off the road, probably aiming for fields of unharvested corn and potatoes. Their movement disrupted Little Crow's plan. The wagons' path took them toward the Dakotas' ambush positions. As they drew near, 20 or so braves rose up and fired at the wagons. The soldiers in the wagons were from the 3rd Minnesota, one of the few veteran units in Sibley's force. Their proficient response surprised the warriors. Firing and reloading by ranks, they returned consistent, accurate fire. They were soon joined by other members of the 3rd who raced from their campsite to join the fray. Far from retreating, they initially pushed forward against the attackers.

As the shooting grew more intense and Dakotas in large numbers moved against the small unit, Sibley ordered them back. The initial encounter soon escalated into a major confrontation as the full Dakota contingent joined the battle, forming a large arc that threatened Sibley's flanks. A hastily put together skirmish line stopped the Indians' frontal charge. Soon after, the Sioux launched a heavy strike along the ravine to the right of Sibley's defenses. He countered with concentrated artillery fire and by shifting an additional unit to the threatened site. As the attackers retreated, Sibley sent six companies to clear the area. Soon after, he dispatched another company to a section on the perimeter under pressure near the lake.

For two hours exceptionally heavy fighting erupted all around Sibley's defensive perimeter. Finally, at about ten o'clock, the Sioux broke off the assault and withdrew. Sibley had gained a decisive victory, although one not without cost. Losses among soldiers were seven killed (one source claims only four) and 33 wounded. Indian losses were thought to be especially heavy with perhaps has many as 30 killed. Rare for them, the Sioux left the bodies of several warriors—at least 14 of them—on the battlefield. Mankato, one of the Dakota's most prominent chiefs, was among those killed. Though not evident at the time, Sibley's men, well supported by effective use of the 6-pound cannon, had achieved a decisive victory in the Minnesota portion of the war.

THE LASTING CONSEQUENCES OF WOOD LAKE

THOUGH OCCASIONAL small raids persisted for a considerable time, the Sioux's defeat at Wood Lake would signal the end of major organized warfare in Minnesota. Sibley's victory set the stage for the subsequent release of captives held by Little Crow's followers.

For two days after the difficult battle, Sibley remained in camp making plans and tending to the wounded. Due to a lack of cavalry, he chose not to engage in close pursuit. He perhaps also feared that a precipitous move might lead to the deaths of the nearly 300 captives. There is indeed some informed conjecture that Little Crow's initial intent following the defeat at Wood Lake was to kill the prisoners.

For the Sioux, though, the catastrophe at Wood Lake changed the dynamic of the war. Dissension inside the tribe had been growing; a sizable contingent led by influential chiefs advocated peace. While Little Crow and his warriors were engaged at Wood Lake, members of the peace party took control of the captives and moved them to their own camp. Prepared to defend against Little Crow's men, instead peace advocates watched many of the hostiles flee to the west, seeking safety in the open prairie beyond Sibley's reach.

For a brief time, Little Crow and some of his closest followers returned to their main camp at Yellow Medicine. Those that did so remained only for a short while—long enough to hurriedly collect family members and retrieve a few essential belongings. Then, they scattered. Shaken and overwhelmed by the extent of their defeat, most were gone before sunset. Before leaving, they handed the small number of captives who had been left behind at Yellow Medicine to members of the peace party.

Little Crow, with a small group, struck out for Canada. Despite extensive efforts to track him down, for the next year the whereabouts of the Dakota leader would remain unknown.

CAMP RELEASE

SIBLEY MOVED SLOWLY toward the Dakota camp, not wishing to risk abrupt movement that might be misinterpreted and jeopardize the captives' safety. In the meantime, the peace delegation sent a message to him indicating that the prisoners were safe and the camp would offer no resistance.

Sibley arrived at the Sioux encampment near Lac qui Parle at about two o'clock in the afternoon on September 26. With a small escort that included drums and a color guard, he walked into camp and entered into negotiations. Two hundred and forty-one captives—among them Sophie Lammers, her two children, and E.W. Earle's mother—were quickly set free at the site that from that day became known as Camp Release. An additional 28 held elsewhere were turned loose the following day. Most in both groups were severely malnourished and some were naked or nearly so. All 269 were subsequently sent under escort to Mankato. Sophie Lammers was eventually taken to Fort Ridgely where she met the Rieke family and where she would renew her acquaintance with August Gluth.

When Sibley's troops occupied the village where the captives had been held, they took about 1,200 tribesmen into custody. In the days that followed, patrols scoured the countryside rounding up others. Some units ventured far to the west into Dakota Territory. Additional groups of Indians came to surrender under flags of truce. Eventually, Sibley's forces at Camp Release held about 2,000 prisoners. Food supplies soon became a problem. On October 4, he sent 1,200 Sioux under guard to gather corn and potatoes from nearby fields. Finally, with local resources exhausted, he sent 1,600 to 1,700 men, women, and children to Fort Snelling.

The Dakotas arrived at the fort on November 13 after an eight-day trek covering about 180 miles. There, they were placed on Pike Island near the confluence of the Mississippi and Minnesota Rivers not far from present-day suburbs of St. Paul. Overlooked by Fort Snelling situated high on an adjoining bluff, the site was thought to afford easier provisioning and offer more secure observation of the tribesmen. For the next several weeks they were housed in tents in an enclosed area on the island. Conditions were difficult; the place was rife with disease and sanitation was lacking. On the way to the fort and later at Mankato where punishments were carried out, soldiers guarding the Indians sometimes had to shield them from attacks by vengeful citizens.

With the release of the captives, Sibley asked to be relieved of his command. In a letter to General Pope, he stated that the objectives of his campaign—to defeat the Indians and free the captives—had been attained. His request was not granted. Instead, on September 29, President Lincoln approved his promotion to brigadier general of volunteers.

HOMECOMING

A MONTH AFTER the Fort Ridgely fighting ended, the Riekes returned to their farm. On their way they found the bodies of John Buechro and his friend who had been killed on August 20, the day of the first attack on the fort. The remains of a Sioux warrior were found nearby.

A pistol, discovered by George Rieke near Buechro's body, remains a treasured possession of the Rieke family.

For a considerable time after their return the Riekes were almost alone in the area. Some family groups had essentially been wiped out during in the uprising. Others were dissuaded from coming back by the still-fresh memories of recent horrors and the occasional isolated attacks that still continued.

In contrast to the homesteads of their neighbors, the Riekes found that their log house and outbuildings had not been burned. Although many items had been taken from their home and they had lost much of their livestock, the family was able to put their lives back together rather quickly.

A letter from George to a brother in Ohio summarized the family's return to the homestead and the circumstances that confronted them on their arrival.

*Thank God, we are all reasonably well. Henry would
not have died as yet had it not been for the battle. He
believed, when he saw someone fall at our cannon, that it
was one of us… He is buried at the fort, but we expect to
remove the body at an early date. Aside from this, none of
the rest of us was injured.*

*At this time we are all home again. We were at the fort
just one month. Frederick fled to St. Peter. The Indians
did not burn any of our property. We still have our wheat,
rye, and barley. We have not yet stacked our oats and
buckwheat. Our beds, tables, chairs and stove, twenty-
two head of cattle, six pigs, five chickens, and a few
cooking utensils we saved. The Indians took with them
or destroyed our best and worthiest clothes, bed clothes,
shirts, towels, sacks, the clock, mirror, razors, pewter
ware, porcelain ware, knives and forks, Mother's sewing
box, Victor's tobacco box, one bull, five pigs, fifty hens,
eleven ducks, our trunk and nearly all small things. The
bull was shot near the fort. Victor has kept his carpenter
tools, and the wagon, plow, harrow, and hay equipment
we still have; and when the Army came to the fort the
soldiers took whatever the Indians left behind. They
took our hay and one hundred bushels of potatoes, and
our onions. We made hay for ourselves again. They say
everything will be paid for. That they can easily do as
the government had to pay 90,000 dollars to the Indians every year {the reference is to the annuity payment,
in actuality $71,000}. The 90,000 dollars for this year
was at the fort. That was a barrel of money that would*

take three men to handle. We can figure that we lost 300 dollars worth of our property. Many of our neighbors lost considerably more, and how many have been murdered, of that we have no idea yet; there must be over one thousand. In the country around New Ulm they are still burying dead almost daily. Near where Mr. Spellbrink lives, they are nearly all murdered. He and his family were saved. From those living above the fort, only four families were rescued. Many families were entirely annihilated. The Indians took away many women. Many people hid themselves, but most of them were killed. The whole county of Renville is gone, many of our acquaintances. Our nearest neighbor {the reference is to John Buechro} was shot near the fort. He together with an older man, both former soldiers, took a wagon on Wednesday morning, the day on which the afternoon battle occurred, to go home and get bedding and other things and were already close to the fort when they were shot… It can hardly be described how horribly people were killed. Children were taken out of their cradles and hung up by their feet. The hands of some men were first chopped off, the chest slashed open and the heart ripped from the body. Enough said of these atrocities. The soldiers are now in pursuit of them, and they are moving ever more westward. We have been told that 500 Indians have been captured and also that fifty white women and children have been taken from the Indians. More than probable William Lammers' wife and children are among them. Our former governor is the commander.

While there is no way of confirming it, Rieke family lore suggests that they were spared the harshest treatment because of the kindness they had shown toward the Sioux and the family's friendship with members of the tribe—a friendship attested to by the gift of the pipestone peace pipe. According to this view, that relationship also perhaps explained their unmolested travel on the first day of the fighting and Victor's escape under fire while hauling water to Fort Ridgely.

Whatever the circumstances that might have played a part in it, the family had survived. For the Riekes the war was over.

Throughout the surviving settler population, homecomings were especially poignant. For those who had experienced the deaths of parents and siblings, the emotions were strong and sometimes conflicting. Some simply wanted to get on with life. Others, though, sought retribution. Minnie Buce's older brother, who had been held captive after having seen his parents and three siblings killed by the Sioux, was determined to avenge their deaths. Family tradition has it that in his quest for revenge August later joined the army and was killed with Custer at the Little Bighorn. (Though it is quite possible he joined the Army, official records do not list a casualty by that name being killed during the battle.)

Similarly, Eusebius and Emanuel, surviving sons of the Reyff family who also resided in Flora Township, took up arms after their parents and two siblings were killed by the Sioux on the morning of August 18. Emanuel witnessed the deaths of his family members and somehow managed to escape to Fort Ridgely. Eusebius was away from home that morning at work on a farm near New Ulm.

Both Eusebius and Emanuel enlisted in Company K of the 7th Minnesota. Their first assignment was particularly daunting: They were sent into the countryside to bury the dead. When their duties brought them to the Reyff homestead, only the bones of their father, mother, sister, and brother remained. They buried the family members in a common grave near the garden.

A further duty at Mankato soon awaited them.

PROCEEDINGS AT MANKATO

WITH HUNDREDS of Dakotas in custody, government authorities met to decide on next steps. Securing approval from senior officials, the military began a screening process intended to identify those who actively participated in the uprising. Sibley appointed a five-member tribunal to take testimony, sift through evidence, and pass judgment on individual cases.

The panel began work on September 28 and concluded on November 5, after hearing testimony from soldiers, former captives, tradesmen and settlers who survived the raids; and members of the Dakota peace party. One of those who testified before the tribunal was August Gluth, who in his six weeks as a captive had been an eyewitness to several killings. In his testimony, he identified two Sioux who were eventually convicted.

Although the numbers vary a bit depending on the source, most accounts place the total number tried at 392. Of those convicted, 16 were given prison terms and 303 were sentenced to death.

While the climate of the times was such that the verdicts enjoyed general support among the populace and media, some concerned citizens—foremost among them Episcopal

Bishop Henry Whipple—expressed misgivings. Citing conditions in the agencies and the historically poor treatment of the Dakotas by government agents as factors that contributed to the uprising, Whipple and others appealed for reconsideration. Dismayed by what they considered to be the hurried nature of the tribunal proceedings some, like Whipple, took the issue directly to President Lincoln.

When the panel's results were transmitted to Washington D.C., Lincoln asked the newly-arrived John Pope, who had not been involved in the tribunal, to send the full trial records of all those convicted. Pope immediately complied and Lincoln set two legal scholars to the task of reviewing them. Lincoln's intention was to make a distinction between military belligerents—those who had fought on the battlefield—and those who had raped and murdered. Lincoln himself reviewed the records—notable indeed given the extraordinary burdens already thrust upon him as the Union fought for survival. On December 6 Abraham Lincoln took pen in hand and in his neat, cursive handwriting, wrote out the names of 39 Dakotas, taking special care to spell out the English versions of each name. Lincoln's list identified those who were to be hanged.

The condemned men learned of their fate on December 22. The following day they sang and danced and were permitted visits with family. Eventually, 38—those identified by witnesses as having committed rape and wanton murder—were hanged at Mankato on December 26. The day was uncommonly warm for late December in Minnesota. Members of the vast crowd milled around in temperatures so mild there was no need for coats.

The largest mass hanging in American history took place at ten fifteen in the morning in front of hundreds of spectators, one of whom was August Gluth. All were hanged at the same time. The Reyff brothers, Eusebius and Emanuel, who had buried the bones of their parents, brother, and sister in a common grave near the family's garden, were among those who guarded the prisoners. On the day of the hangings, Emanuel's name was drawn by lottery to place the noose around the neck of one of the condemned men. Some accounts state that the family of the hangman, Joseph Daly, was among those killed in the uprising. After being left dangling on the scaffold for a half hour or so, the bodies of the 38 who had been hanged were cut down, hauled away, and eventually placed in a shallow grave on a sandbar near the Minnesota River. Before daybreak of the following morning, in a practice not uncommon at the time, most of the bodies had been dug up and taken by physicians for use as medical cadavers.

On Christmas night, as the 39 Sioux prisoners awaited their fate the following morning, one, a Dakota elder named Round Wind, was reprieved. During the evening, a dispatch was received from the President countermanding the order for Round Wind's execution.

The reasons for reversing the order are not entirely clear. Apparently, though, factors surfaced surrounding the case that cast a degree of doubt on Round Wind's guilt. August Gluth had testified against Round Wind, asserting that he was only twenty paces away when he saw the Indian kill a settler. Gluth's young companion, who had also tended Little Crow's ponies and been a prisoner of the Sioux for many weeks, told the tribunal that Round Wind had shot his mother. However, several women who the two youngsters thought could corroborate their testimony were unable to identify the prisoner.

Round Wind had professed his innocence, saying that he was on the other side of the Minnesota River at the time the killings occurred. A medical doctor and missionary, Dr. Thomas Williamson, stated that after the war started Round Wind had taken a starving five-year old, the child of a slain settler, and had sheltered and nourished her until she recovered. Round Wind reportedly attended weekly worship services on a regular basis and was baptized by Williamson a few days prior to his scheduled hanging. Williamson also asserted that his brother-in-law, Stephen Riggs, also a Protestant missionary, had seen Round Wind after the war started and had not been harmed or threatened by him.

There may have been other considerations as well. Subsequent research indicated that Round Wind's sister was married to Joseph Renville, an influential local trader (Minnesota's Renville County is named for him). Conceivably, that connection might have contributed in some way to the outcome, perhaps by providing sufficient leverage for the case to be examined in more detail. It is also possible that Lincoln did not wish to consign an individual to the gallows based on the primary testimony of two very young boys—especially when associated information painted a more shaded picture of events.

In the days that followed, several prisoners were given pardons due to a lack of evidence. The 264 prisoners whose death sentences had been commuted by the President were held in Minnesota through the winter of 1862–63. In the spring, they were transferred to Camp McClellan in Davenport, Iowa. Most were incarcerated there for the next four years. Considerable numbers died of disease during their confinement. Survivors were eventually released to join their families in Nebraska, many of whom had been expelled earlier from Minnesota.

BANISHMENT

THE DEMANDS of outraged citizens terrified by the hundreds of deaths and appalled by the stories of atrocities, fueled pressure to remove Natives from Minnesota. Subsequently, over the next months, almost all, including peace party advocates and members of non-Sioux tribes, would be sent west to Dakota Territory. A small number, judged to be "friendly," were allowed to remain. Several would later serve as scouts for Sibley on his later campaigns.

Indeed, for the white citizens of Minnesota, the feelings of terror evoked by the uprising and the images of the carnage that resulted from it would remain in the state's collective consciousness for years to come. The immediate effect, though, was to seek the expulsion of the Native population from the state. Fanned by an excited press, there was little attempt to differentiate "hostiles" from friendly Indians. Governor Ramsey urged that Natives "be driven forever beyond the boundaries of the state."

Influenced by political leaders such as Ramsey, Congress appropriated funds taken from annuity money to reimburse victims of the attacks. Legislation removing the Winnebagos from the state was enacted on February 21, 1863. A similar statute involving the Sioux was passed on March

3. Provisions specified that the tribes were to be relocated beyond the limits of any state and that the sale of their old reservation lands be reinvested for the tribes' benefit. Fifty thousand dollars in additional monies were allocated to assist in the relocation of both tribes.

After several tribulations and journeys by steamboat and on foot, most of the Sioux were eventually placed on Crow Creek Reserve in present day South Dakota. After similar difficulties, the Winnebagos were also transported to Crow Creek.

The location proved unsatisfactory to both tribes. The landscape was dismal and not well suited for agriculture. The two groups disliked each other intensely. Historic animosities and memories of violence between them persisted. In combination, the arduous journey, inhospitable locale, and intertribal strife caused widespread suffering and numerous deaths among the tribal populations. Rather soon, large numbers of Winnebagos began migrating to the Omaha Reservation in Nebraska where by a later treaty they were allowed to remain.

Three years later, after Crow Creek had proven unsatisfactory for raising crops, the remaining population of Sioux was transferred to the Santee Reservation near the mouth of the Niobrara River in Nebraska.

Meanwhile, after departing Minnesota, bands primarily from the Upper Sioux Agency roamed the Dakota plains for several years before, in 1867, being gathered on reservations at Devil's Lake in present-day North Dakota and at Sisseton in present-day South Dakota. Eventually, over the years, small numbers began trickling back to Minnesota.

NEXT STEPS

BANISHMENT OF SIOUX tribesmen from the state would not close the chapter on the Sioux Uprising or end the major war that resulted from it.

Though some smaller localized attacks would continue at least into 1865, Sibley's victory at Wood Lake brought major fighting within Minnesota to a close. The power of the greater Sioux nation had not been broken, however. Though some of it was undoubtedly exaggerated, ominous news of buildups of Sioux warriors southwest of the Missouri River in Dakota Territory brought the possibility of renewed fighting in the spring.

To establish a defensive perimeter and allay continuing fears, Sibley and Pope established posts along two crescent-shaped defensive lines running from Fort Abercrombie east and south to the Iowa border. Shock from the recent cataclysmic events persisted, however. The thought of thousands of free-ranging hostiles in Dakota Territory and possibilities of further attacks were more than citizens and political leaders cared to contemplate.

Convinced that the Sioux would stage attacks along the Minnesota frontier during the following summer, General Pope planned a two-pronged expedition into Dakota

Territory. General Sibley would lead one column, mostly infantry, north to Devil's Lake in present-day North Dakota. General Alfred Sully would take a cavalry-dominated wing up the Missouri River Valley before swinging north to meet Sibley.

SIBLEY'S 1863 CAMPAIGN

SIBLEY, WITH A FORCE of nearly 3,300 departed from a camp near present-day Redwood Falls on June 16, 1863. Moving in a column five miles long and traveling at times from two o'clock in the morning until noon to avoid the blistering heat, the difficult, month-long trek took Sibley to a point about 40 miles southeast of Devil's Lake. There, scouts advised him that a large assemblage of Sioux had recently left Devil's Lake and headed generally west toward the Missouri River. Early on July 20, Sibley set out after them with a force of about 2,000 infantry, 800 cavalry, 150 artillerymen and associated scouts. Sibley took with him 225 mule-drawn wagons carrying supplies for three months and 100 wagons filled with ammunition and equipment. It was the largest body of troops ever sent against the Indians in the Upper Missouri River region. Four days later a patrol sighted Indians moving across the prairie toward a large village not far away.

Sibley halted and made camp while Sioux tribesmen watched from a range of hills about a mile distant. The largest band was positioned on the highest knoll, called Big Mound, in present-day Kidder County, North Dakota. The battle commenced when from the midst of warriors riding towards Sibley's camp, a young warrior shot one of the surgeons accompanying the column.

The Sioux attacked in considerable numbers—perhaps as many as 1,500—and fought until late afternoon, before Sibley's numbers and firepower forced them to break off the battle. Their retreat took them westward, followed immediately by Sibley whose close pursuit resulted in a running fight that lasted until darkness set in. Two days later he caught up with the Sioux. Making effective use of cannon to disperse large clusters of Sioux horsemen, he beat them again at an encounter near Dead Buffalo Lake. On July 28, two days after the Dead Buffalo Lake engagement, Sibley inflicted a major defeat on the Sioux at Stony Lake, northwest of present-day Driscoll, North Dakota. At Stony Lake, Sioux in enormous numbers attacked Sibley's force as it was breaking camp. Arrayed in a vast semicircle, a mounted column five to six miles across faced Sibley's troopers. Shifting forces and using cannon until his wagons were laagered, Sibley routed the attackers, forcing them across the Missouri. The hasty withdrawal and Sibley's unremitting pressure caused the Sioux to abandon many of their carts and travois, as well as dried meat, tallow, robes, cooking utensils, and camp paraphernalia.

Sibley lost three killed and four wounded, one of whom died later. Sioux losses are uncertain. The tribe's oral history mentions 24 warriors killed in the three battles. Conversely, one Minnesota regiment alone claimed as many as 31 slain out of a possible total of 150.

Sibley pressed on the following day, July 29, reaching the east bank of the Missouri in the vicinity of present-day

Bismarck, North Dakota. He waited for a time without result for Sully's column to join him. Then, with supplies running low he returned to Fort Snelling, reaching there on September 13.

Meanwhile, during the campaign, welcome news had come in July to Sibley's column and, indeed, to the white residents of Minnesota. Little Crow, the major Sioux leader during the uprising, had been killed. After initially escaping to Canada, he had sneaked back across the border on a horse-stealing raid. On July 3, he was shot and killed by a settler.

ALFRED SULLY

ALFRED SULLY WAS a slender officer of medium height. His distinguished appearance was made notable by a thin face framed by dark hair and a long, narrow beard that extended to the top button of his tunic. In his later years, the "salt and pepper" in his beard added further character to his appearance. In addition to being a competent military commander, Sully was a gifted artist. The son of a nationally-known portrait painter, Sully's watercolors—many of them painted while serving at duty stations on the Great Plains and Pacific Northwest—grace the displays of galleries throughout the country.

Sully brought considerable experience in Indian warfare to his new assignment as a subordinate to General Pope. For seven years beginning in 1854, he commanded forces across the central plains at Fort Pierre, Fort Kearny, and Fort Ridgely in Dakota Territory, Nebraska Territory and Minnesota, respectively. Clashes with the Sioux and Northern Cheyenne added to Indian-fighting experience gained in California and Oregon during earlier service in the Pacific Northwest.

A different form of service would subsequently occupy Sully's attention. Within a month after Fort Sumter, the

U.S. flag was torn off the post office at St. Joseph, Missouri, and trampled by a secessionist mob. Later in the summer of 1861, Confederate militia took control of the town. Sully led Union forces from Fort Leavenworth, Kansas, and in September occupied the city, declared martial law, and put down persisting violence.

Along with many other veteran officers based on the plains, Sully was called east as the fighting intensified. Appointed colonel in the 1st Minnesota Volunteer Infantry in March 1862, he served for a brief time manning defenses around Washington, D.C., and then led units during the Seven Days Battle, Antietam, and Fredericksburg. His performance at Antietam on September 17 earned him command of a brigade and promotion to brigadier general of volunteers.

In the spring of 1863, Sully was removed from command and returned to duty in the West. The stated reason for his dismissal was an alleged inability to control a near-mutinous regiment of New York infantry. There was, however, speculation that his identification as a "McClellan man"—sympathetic to, if not supportive of, General George McClellan—may have contributed to his removal by superiors wary of officers with known linkages to the controversial former commander of the Army of the Potomac.

Sully was disheartened by the transfer. Nonetheless, the timing and location of his new posting were propitious. He was immediately engaged in combatting the Sioux on grounds familiar to him in Minnesota and Dakota. The assignment was militarily sound as well: Sully's experience with Plains Indians far surpassed that of most of his contemporaries.

Pope's campaign plan called for Sully's command to move north up the Missouri River while Sibley pushed from southwest Minnesota into Dakota Territory. Pope intended that the two converging wings would form a pincer, trapping the Sioux. While the full plan never reached fruition, the series of successful clashes led by Sibley and a victory by Sully at Whitestone Hill reduced the immediate threat to the Minnesota frontier.

Much to the displeasure of General Pope, Sully's departure was delayed by low water levels on the Missouri that prevented travel by steamboat. Prodded by Pope, Sully began his expedition on August 21, 1863, initially moving north along the Missouri River with a force of about 1,900 men. The bulk of Sully's striking power was supplied by the 6th Iowa Cavalry commanded by Colonel David Wilson and the 2nd Nebraska Cavalry led by Colonel Robert Furnas, plus assorted scouts and artillery. After leaving one company of the 2nd Nebraska at Fort Randall, the first in a chain of forts on the Upper Missouri just north of the Dakota-Nebraska border, Sully followed the river angling west and north until the column reached Fort Pierre in August.

At Fort Pierre, almost in the center of present-day South Dakota, Sully rested and replenished his force. On the 13th, he again took the field moving generally north. He took with him about 1,200 men, the remainder having been left to garrison outposts along the way or placed on patrol duty. Sully was a prudent officer, known for security and discipline while on the march. On September 3, scouts discovered a large Sioux village of about 400 lodges housing 2,000 to

4,000 Indians, at Whitestone Hill, 23 miles southeast of present-day Kulm, North Dakota.

The encampment housed Indians from several Sioux tribal groups—Santee, Yankton, and Teton—some of whom had fled the fighting in Minnesota or had been pushed to the region by General Sibley's column. It was late afternoon when the scouts' report reached Sully who was riding with the main column about 10 miles away. Sully quickly dispatched an advance force of about 300 men, directing their commander, Major A. E. House, to surround the camp and, if possible, prevent the Sioux from scattering. After assigning four companies to guard his supply train, Sully then hurried toward the village with his main force of 600 to 700 cavalrymen.

At about six o'clock, Sully reached high ground overlooking the Indian camp. The large, dispersed village spread out on the prairie before him. Seeing movement in the village and tepees being torn down, he sent the 6th Iowa to the right and the 2nd Nebraska to the left to close off ravines that afforded concealment and escape routes for the Sioux. After both flanks were covered, Sully, with three companies and artillery, moved straight into the village. Because of the close-in chaotic nature of the fighting that followed, Sully's artillery was never used. Initial resistance was scattered and considerable numbers of Sioux surrendered as Sully advanced.

Fighting flared up on the flanks, however, and grew in violence as Sioux warriors were caught between the Iowans on one side and the Nebraskans on the other. Advancing on foot, the Iowa unit pressed the Sioux towards the 2nd

Nebraska, a unit Sully later complimented for its marksmanship. Both cavalry regiments were equipped with infantry rifles rather than their normal carbines, thus increasing the range and lethality of their weapons. Firing from as close as 60 yards, the cavalrymen exacted a heavy toll on their attackers.

As darkness approached, in a poorly conducted charge led by Colonel Wilson the Iowa regiment was beaten back and both sides hunkered down for the night. Wary of friendly fire prospects and losing communication with his soldiers in the dark, Colonel Furnas pulled his Nebraska troops back slightly to a more favorable defensive position in the rolling terrain.

During the night, most of the Indians abandoned the camp. The Sioux did not entirely flee the area, however, and for the next two days skirmishes, sometimes heavy, continued as they fought to retake the village or regain their possessions. On September 5, a 27-man patrol collided with 300 or more Sioux about 15 miles from the battle site. The cavalrymen were forced into a fighting retreat, losing six killed and one wounded. Meanwhile, Sully's troops destroyed the village and its contents, burning perhaps as much as a half million pounds of dried buffalo meat, the Indians' cache of winter provisions.

Altogether, Sully's casualties probably amounted to 20 to 22 killed and 38 wounded. Estimates of Sioux losses varied widely, ranging from 100 to 300 with another 150 or more captured. Rare in frontier casualty reports, the Indians' estimates of their own casualties were as high or higher than those suggested by the cavalrymen. Some tribesmen guessed that as many as 300 had been killed or wounded and another 250 taken prisoner. Clearly, it was a devastating loss for the Sioux.

Native losses included an unknown number of women and children, prompting some critics to label the battle as a massacre. Dissenters noted the similarities in clothing worn by Sioux warriors and women and argued that most were killed in the chaotic jumble of the fight inside the village. Finally, the large number of cavalry losses (although some may have resulted from friendly fire) did not bespeak of a massacre.

Their extended time in the field had left Sully and his troopers low on supplies. With wounded to care for and horses and mules played out, he left Whitestone Hill on September 6 and returned to Fort Pierre. Nearby, he built a new fort, Fort Sully, and quartered there with much of his command through the winter of 1863–64.

1864: THE DECISIVE YEAR

THOUGH SIBLEY'S VICTORY at Wood Lake in late 1862 and Sibley's and Sully's successes in 1863 had pushed much of the threat away from Minnesota's borders, Pope and his generals recognized that the results were less complete than intended. The capability of the Sioux nation to wage destructive war remained largely intact. Rumors of Sioux plans to block river traffic and attack emigrant trains and settlements further abetted underlying fears. Recollections of August 1862 were still vivid in the memories of Minnesota citizens—and would remain there for years.

Pope responded by requesting more cavalry to go after the nomadic bands and by planning a campaign that would take the battle to the Sioux. The 1864 expeditions would again send Henry Sibley and Alfred Sully into Indian territory.

Sully would traverse farthest west, moving across present-day North Dakota and, for a time, into eastern Montana. On July 28, 1864, at Killdeer Mountain in western North Dakota, his innovative tactics thoroughly defeated the Sioux in what may have been the largest single engagement between U.S. Army forces and Native tribes ever fought on American soil. Sully then pursued the Sioux bands, forcing them farther west and beating them again in a prolonged running battle labelled the Battle of the Badlands.

Operations began in the spring. Pope's notion for the campaign was to shield settlers from attacks that persisted, although in Minnesota the raids were neither of the size nor the frequency of previous years. Ordered by Pope to establish a string of forts along the Missouri River, Sully pushed a sizable force west across present-day North Dakota and into the area of the Little Yellowstone.

A second purpose of Sully's expedition was to protect lines of communication to gold fields newly discovered in Montana and Idaho. The most direct route for the ore, badly needed by the Union, was via steamboat on the Missouri River through Sioux territory. On June 28, as Sully's forces were on the march, three Indians killed a topographical engineer who was collecting specimens while accompanying Sully's column. After an advance element of troopers chased and killed the three warriors, Sully, a man of considerable temper, had the corpses decapitated and the heads mounted on stakes as a warning to other hostile tribesmen.

The full campaign came together the following day, June 29, when a 1,700-man contingent having followed the Missouri River from Sioux City, Iowa, joined a second column of 1,550 soldiers who marched overland from Fort Ridgely. Eight days after the units joined, Sully established a new post, Fort Rice, 30 miles south of present-day Mandan, North Dakota, as a base for the expedition. Steamboats were chartered to transport supplies and support the force as it moved. Alerted by scouts to the presence of a massive encampment 130 miles northwest, Sully left Fort Rice on

July 19. Forced to devote some of his manpower to convoy a wagon train of 200 miners and families, Sully took with him about 2,200 men supported by two artillery batteries and eight howitzers. On July 26, a week into the march, Sully's scouts skirmished with a large party of Sioux near present-day Richardton, North Dakota. One scout was wounded in the struggle. Convinced that the Sioux now knew of his presence, Sully moved quickly, covering as much as 47 miles on the day before the battle. In the early morning hours of July 28, Sully's chief scout reported sighting an immense Sioux village with perhaps as many as 1,600 lodges, about 10 miles away.

The site of the encampment was along the east rim of the Dakota Badlands. Aptly named, the landscape, torn by eons of wind and water erosion, was cleft by sharp crevasses, dry washes, and jagged outcroppings. Realizing that the fractured ground was not conducive to cavalry, Sully devised a marvelously innovative tactic: he dismounted his cavalrymen and formed them into a massive hollow square, a mile and a quarter long on each side. Sheltered inside the square were his horses and artillery, giving the latter freedom to shift inside the moving formation to cover areas most under threat. As standard practice, one trooper out of every four moved in back of the line, holding mounts for his squad mates. Making effective use of his rifles, which out-ranged the Indians' weapons, Sully moved the enormous square toward the village.

Shots were first exchanged at long range before the Sioux began probing the sides of the formation, singly at the outset, then in small groups, and finally in larger contingents. All such threats were beaten back, helped by artillery fire that broke up the larger masses of warriors.

As the square pushed inexorably forward, a Sioux attempt to shatter the formation with an attack on the trailing edge was blown apart by an artillery shell that exploded in the midst of several on-rushing warriors. Charges followed against both the left and right sides of the square. Both were defeated with losses. On the right, Sully's men leaped into saddles and mounted a counter-charge. Supported by fire from a battery of howitzers, the tactic scattered the Yankton and Santee attackers. The cavalrymen chased and caught a band of fleeing warriors, piling into them with sabers and side arms. One trooper was killed in the melee.

It was late afternoon, nearly dark, when Sully reached the village. He broke off the attack but ringed the village with artillery and bombarded it through the night. Some warriors fought delaying actions, but most of the camp's inhabitants fled, leaving tepees and possessions behind.

The next day Sully ordered the destruction of the contents of the village. Tepees, buffalo meat, blankets and other possessions were burned. Weapons were destroyed and holes were punched in cooking pots and pans. Other utensils were damaged beyond repair. Perhaps as many as 3,000 dogs, used to pull travois as well as for food, were shot. Some contemporary reports suggest that before they could be stopped, early arriving Winnebago scouts, bitter enemies of the Sioux, killed an unknown number of adults and children who had been left behind.

The majority of the Sioux fled west from Killdeer Mountain deeper into the Badlands. Some remained behind, though, and for a few days harassed the column. The night after the battle, two of Sully's pickets were killed and another wounded by a small party of raiders. The following night another was killed by friendly fire, likely induced by frayed nerves.

The battle and its immediate aftermath cost Sully five dead and ten wounded. Sully estimated Sioux casualties at 100 to 150 killed. The Indians acknowledged 31 dead.

Killdeer Mountain was a massive encounter waged over a landscape covering several miles. The engagement likely involved the largest number of combatants — 2,200 soldiers and an estimated 1,600 or more Indian warriors — of any battle in the American West. Perhaps because of the relatively small number of casualties and the fact that it was not decisive in the long-term, neither the battle itself nor Sully's exceptional tactics are well remembered.

Sully was subsequently joined on the march by the 800 soldiers he had earlier left to guard the civilian wagon train. With his command now bulked up to 3,000 soldiers, Sully pushed west through the Badlands' innumerable gullies and clay ridges. On August 7, his column was attacked deep in the Badlands near present-day Medora, North Dakota, by large numbers of Sioux. What later became known as the Battle of the Badlands was really a three-day running skirmish — a series of attacks, charges, counter-charges, and spasm exchanges — that left 13 troopers dead or wounded. Sully later estimated that the Sioux suffered 100 casualties or more, but most modern scholars believe the tribe's losses were considerably less.

The battle began in earnest in the early morning hours of August 7 when Sioux raiders attempted to capture or scatter the 7th Iowa Cavalry's horse herd. Soon after, one of the regiment's companies was ambushed. Later in the day, hundreds of warriors lined hilltops near Sully's main camp before being dispersed by artillery fire.

On August 8, terrain features forced the column into narrow defiles, stretching it out over three or four miles. At times during the day, an estimated 1,000 Sioux showered arrows on the cavalrymen, firing from bluffs at the front and along the sides of the constricted passages. Sully defended successfully, using cannon fire and cavalry charges to push back the attackers. Despite the opposition from warriors swirling around the flanks, the column moved about 10 miles during the day.

August 9 began with a reprise of the previous days' activities. This time the action was focused near the front of the column where masses of Indians on high ground unsuccessfully attempted to disrupt Sully's advance. At mid-day, the column finally cleared the Badlands, breaking out into a broad, level plain. The open expanse gave Sully room to maneuver. Free to deploy his artillery and with his cavalry now unobstructed, Sully quickly dispersed the tribesmen. Soon after, scouts found the remainder of a large, recently occupied village. The Sioux had scattered in all directions. The battle was over.

On August 12, the column reached the Yellowstone River where two steamboats were waiting with 50 tons of supplies. Convinced that he had pushed most of the hostiles into Montana, Sully dispatched 900 troops—600 infantry and dismounted cavalry and 300 cavalry—from Fort Rice to rescue a cavalry unit and members of an emigrant train trapped 160 miles away near present-day Marmarth, North Dakota. A Hunkpapa Sioux war party that included Sitting Bull, who was wounded in the fight, had attacked and surrounded the dug-in troopers. Sully's relief force arrived in time to break the siege, although not before casualties had been sustained by both sides.

SIBLEY'S CONTRIBUTIONS: 1864

HENRY SIBLEY HAD a busy year in 1864. Although his activities were less visible and not on the same scale as those of his colleague Alfred Sully, they contributed in a substantial way to the pacification of southwestern Minnesota and the settlements along the western border.

Named commander of the Military District of Minnesota, Sibley's continued involvement building and improving fortifications that ran from Dakota Territory down the western edge of Minnesota and into northern Iowa, helped stabilize the frontier. Main units with headquarters elements were posted at Fort Snelling (6th Minnesota), Mankato (7th Minnesota), Fort Ripley (8th Minnesota), Fort Ridgely (9th Minnesota) and Le Sueur (10th Minnesota). Smaller outposts were positioned elsewhere between major installations and assigned designated patrol areas. Although fears would persist, the outposts eased lingering concerns regarding the potential for sudden major attacks in the future.

In August 1864, rumors of unrest among the Chippewas, perhaps incited by disaffected Sioux, reached departmental headquarters. Sibley sent a small contingent of soldiers to calm settlers near the tribal region along the

Wisconsin-Minnesota border. At the same time, he denied military protection to whiskey traders. In combination, those measures quieted the restiveness.

THE CONTINUING CONFLICT

THE UPRISING in Minnesota and the war against the Sioux in Dakota Territory formed an early chapter in a longer saga played out on an enormous stage. After the fighting subsided in the conflict that began when the four young Dakota braves killed five people at the Robinson Jones farm in Acton Township, wars of varying sizes, lengths, and intensities continued for more than two decades. The conflict area spanned approximately 1,815,640 square miles—more than half of the land mass of the lower continental United States. All or parts of 17 states now shape the immense territory.

For several years prior to the uprising, conditions along the frontier had been relatively quiet. In September 1855, General William S. Harney defeated a sizable band of Oglala and Brule Sioux near present-day Lewellen, Nebraska. The Battle of the Blue Water, as the fight became known, culminated the government's first military expedition against the Plains Indians. Harney's victory was decisive and succeeded in halting raids along the Overland Trail for much of the next decade.

With the Minnesota Uprising, conditions began to change. Relationships between whites and Natives were altered in a more pronounced way following the massacre of Cheyenne tribesmen at Sand Creek, Colorado, in November 1864. At Sand Creek, Colonel John Chivington, an avowed racist who spoke of wading in Indian blood and openly advocated exterminating the Native tribes, led a force of generally undisciplined Colorado militia in an attack on a peaceful Cheyenne village. Many of those killed by Chivington's men were women and children whose body parts were later paraded through the streets of Denver. Chivington's actions outraged the tribes of the Great Plains and turned a war against the Sioux and Cheyenne into a larger war against the Plains Indians.

Throughout the period, atrocities were rampant on both sides. Indeed, Sand Creek must be considered along with the Cherokee "Trail of Tears" as being among the saddest, darkest moments in American history.

The events and personalities associated with the Indian wars of the west are not easily characterized. For every commander like Chivington there are others like George Crook who studied, understood, and respected the Native culture. Indeed, it was Crook who helped orchestrate the proceedings that led to the court case regarding the Ponca chief Standing Bear. The court's decision that Native Americans are persons within the meaning of the law and "have the right of *habeas corpus*" was a seminal event in the history of the United States.

Among the Indians, the presence of merciless killers like Inkpaduta was often balanced by personages such as Logan Fontenelle, an Omaha chief widely respected by his white neighbors. In his later years, Red Cloud, the great Oglala war chief, became a powerful, articulate spokesman for peace.

There were, in both cultures, courageous individuals such as John Other Day who saved the lives of 62 white settlers and Bishop Henry Whipple whose efforts helped persuade President Lincoln to mitigate the sentences of scores of Dakota warriors who had participated in the uprising.

The two decades following the end of the Civil War in 1865 saw conflict spread across the Central Plains, the West, Southwest, and Pacific Northwest. While identical sets of circumstances seldom existed, several frequently recurring conditions served as triggers for many of the wars. These factors varied in intensity from region to region and conflict to conflict. Foremost among them were the westward migration of the nation's growing population—a journey that took thousands of emigrants across Native regions; the discovery of gold or silver on historically Native or treaty land; and farther west on the Plains and in the Southwest, the rapid destruction of the continent's two great bison herds.

The government's attempts to address the "Indian problem" by relocating the tribes or moving them to reservations were often resisted by the free-roaming and fiercely independent tribal groups. The Natives who signed treaties and moved to agencies sometimes faced an additional irritant: as was the case at the Minnesota agencies, government functionaries did not always supply the annuities promised in treaty provisions.

Indeed, treaty violations (sometimes in response to incidents perpetrated by the other party) were not unknown on either side. Native actions most often took the form of thefts of livestock and killing raids on homesteads, settlements, outposts, and emigrant travelers.

The conflicts on the Great Plains and in the West and Southwest would present the U.S. Army with a different form of warfare than its officers and men had experienced during the Civil War. They would face difficult opponents — superb horsemen infused with a warrior culture that sprang from incessant warfare with rival tribes.

At the time the conflicts were most intense, the Native population in the area from the central Plains to the Pacific Coast probably numbered 225,000 — 250,000. Not all were nomadic or hostile. Those that were, however, made formidable adversaries. Tenacious and aggressive, Native warriors formed what may have been "the finest light cavalry in history." The war chiefs were familiar with terrain features and water sources across an immense region that often had yet to see a white surveyor or a rudimentary depiction on a map.

To confront the challenge posed by the hostile tribes and carry out the government's policies, military leaders had access to an Army that even in the immediate aftermath of the Civil War was never large and whose effective strength in the West was further drained by the commitment of sizable numbers of soldiers to Reconstruction duty in the South.

During the 25-year period following the Civil War, the U.S. Army often numbered less than 25,000 officers and men. Those few soldiers manned the nation's 150 forts, posts, camps, arsenals, and armories; guarded 6,000 miles of frontier and coastline; escorted wagon trains, stage coaches, and survey parties; shielded the construction of railroads, trails, and bridges; protected settlers and settlements; scouted; and when called upon, fought Indians. During the full course of the Indian wars, they were called upon to do that more than a thousand times.

Finally, it ended. In 1886, Geronimo's surrender with his last small band of Apaches is generally regarded as the closing event in the series of wars fought by the United States Army against organized, free-roaming groups of Native warriors. In contrast, the tragedy at Wounded Knee in 1890 was an isolated encounter resulting from a terribly mishandled confrontation. In October 1895, a small outbreak occurred at—ironically—Leech Lake, Minnesota. That encounter is considered to be the last Native uprising in the continental United States. Adding further irony to the episode is that Timothy Sheehan, a hero at Fort Ridgely 33 years before, was wounded in the battle.

RETROSPECTIVE

1864 SAW THE LAST of the major campaigns tied directly to the Minnesota Uprising. Left as a result were a string of forts across Dakota Territory. The end of the Civil War brought a further, brief, influx of troops into the territory where many of them would remain until their terms of enlistment expired. Soon settlers by the thousands would arrive, establishing homes and businesses in areas now increasingly open for settlement.

For the residents of Minnesota, the memories and fears associated with events during August and September 1862 would remain part of the state's fabric. Other than monuments and memorial plaques, few tangible reminders of the conflagration remain. The burned buildings are long gone, in many cases replaced by marvels of modern architecture. Towns and settlements once destroyed now thrive again. Blood-soaked soil is now peacefully turned by plows; its fertility matched by few places on the planet.

Although a specific date cannot be assigned to the moment when the pendulum swung from war to peace, for Minnesota, and for the nation, the absence of war on the frontier was a watershed event. The legacy of families like the Riekes and the soldiers, settlers, and Native Americans who rode through the state's history—told in stories of courage, terror, bloodshed, fortitude, and heroism—reach across the decades to surprise, inspire, and instruct the generations that have followed and those that are yet to come.

AFTERWORD

FAMILY TIES

The end of hostilities in the local area found much of the Rieke family, Sophie Lammers, and August Gluth at Fort Ridgely. Thrown together by circumstance, ties among them would flourish, binding them together in a connection that persists to this day.

In the spring of 1864, George Rieke married Sophie Lammers. The two of them had met at the fort. It is uncertain, but possible, that they may have known each other in Ohio before the Rieke and Lammers families moved to Minnesota. Sophie brought to the marriage her two sons who had survived their time in captivity with her. The child that Sophie was carrying during the uprising was born in 1863 but died soon after. George and Sophie would eventually have seven children one of whom, Herman, is the grandfather of Reuben Rieke, one of this book's authors.

At Fort Ridgely, Sophie renewed a friendship with young August Gluth that would last a lifetime. They may have initially met before the uprising when 12-year-old August worked on a nearby farm. They were members of the caravan struck by Little Crow's war party as the group of families fled toward the fort and shared time in captivity together before August's escape.

In 1872, August married Minnie Porth. One of their seven children was a girl named Annie, who later married George and Sophie's son Herman. Annie became Reuben Rieke's grandmother.

THE RIEKES IN LATER YEARS

In the years following the war, the Riekes expanded their farm, raised an increasing variety of crops, and added a flock of 200 sheep. By common consent the home farm went to George. Several other brothers lived and farmed close by. George's brother Victor built a grist mill on a small river near Franklin, Minnesota. A few years later sister Mary and her husband joined Victor in operating the mill. Mary eventually received a pension from the state in recognition of her services at Fort Ridgely. Her name is among those inscribed on the monument that lists the names of the fort's defenders.

George prospered on the farm and developed a combine that was demonstrated at the Brown County Fair. Deeply religious, he donated several acres of his farm to a church building project. With contributions from the Rieke family and their neighbors, a Methodist Church, the first in the area, opened in the 1870s.

In his later years, George began writing poetry. One verse, a paean to America titled "To the Fourth of July," written in old script German, is especially prized by the family. In the fall of 1901, George and Sophie moved to Fairfax, Minnesota. Sophie died there in 1906. George, a must-admired pillar of the community, died September 30, 1926, at age 92.

AUGUST GLUTH

August initially established a homestead near Morgan, Minnesota. Although it was some distance from George and Sophie's farm, the families frequently traded visits, which aided the romance between George and Sophie's son Herman and August's daughter Annie.

August was small in stature. Though well-liked, he was feisty and combative in his dealings, tolerating no insults — real or perceived — directed at himself or any member of his family. As a member of a threshing crew that traveled through the region, he was a frequent participant in the wrestling matches that young crew members engaged in, winning more often than not despite his small size.

August farmed for thirty-five years before moving to Morgan in 1906. After his wife Minnie died in 1908, August began splitting his time between Morgan and Portland, Oregon, where some of his children had settled. In his later years, recalling the moments when he narrowly escaped being killed by tomahawk, he sometimes ruminated on the consequences a few seconds can make in the context of an entire lifetime.

August died on November 22, 1932 at age 82. He is buried in Morgan.

MINNESOTA RIVER VALLEY AND THE NATIVE POPULATION

Settlements in the valley remained mostly empty of population for a considerable time after the devastating events of 1862. New Ulm, a seat of commerce, was a bit of an exception in that small numbers of residents began trickling back to the burned and abandoned city within a few weeks. There and at other locations the rising tide of returnees gained further momentum after the Civil War ended. By the mid-1870s, the valley was once again thriving.

After major fighting ceased in Minnesota in late 1862, most Sioux tribesmen, regardless of which side they had taken during the war, were expelled from the state. A small number were allowed to remain, many of whom scouted for Generals Sibley and Sully during their later campaigns. However, some who actively helped the whites during the war—such as Chief Stuck by the Ree, who had deployed warriors to defend settlers—were also deported.

Eventually, Sioux families began returning, at first in small but eventually increasing numbers. The Lower Sioux Indian Community, one of four federally recognized tribes in Minnesota, was later established with headquarters near Morton, Minnesota. In 1938, 746 acres of original Sioux land near Granite Falls were returned to the tribe and the Upper Sioux Indian Reservation Community was established. Subsequent additions have brought the present-day size to 1,440 acres.

LITTLE CROW

Little Crow was a complex personality. His outward attempts to assimilate—he built a home, sometimes wore white settler clothing, and on the morning of August 17, the day the first settlers were murdered, attended Episcopal services at the Lower Sioux Agency—and serve as a bridge between cultures were often inconsistent and regarded with suspicion by both the white community and fellow tribesmen. Though apparently not initially disposed towards war, he became an implacable foe. He was noted by some for intervening to save lives and denounced by others for the cold-blooded killings in which he was a direct participant. His treatment of captives was also varied widely. He protected some while seeking out others for less than charitable purposes.

As a captive of the Sioux, August Gluth observed Little Crow during the most critical six weeks of the uprising. Though Little Crow had spared his life (admittedly because August provided good care for the chief's prized ponies), Gluth was unremitting in his condemnation of the Sioux leader:

> *Little Crow was a murderous killer and a cruel master. While he urged his subordinate chiefs into daring exploits and cursed them for their failures, he had not the courage to endanger himself very much. He was also vainglorious and a great showman. He enjoyed bedecking himself in the colorful regalia which only a chief could don and he relished the obedience which sub-chiefs and his retinue showed him. He always had a string of ponies of striking appearances and insisted on having them well groomed.*

After the debacle at Wood Lake, Little Crow with initially about 150 followers is thought to have spent the winter near Devil's Lake in present-day northeastern North Dakota. After subsequently fleeing to Canada, Little Crow and others, including his son Wowinapa, returned—how many times is uncertain—on horse-stealing forays. In June of 1863, he, along with his son and a group of 16 others, was again in Minnesota stealing horses and murdering several persons in the process. In the evening of July 3, Little Crow and Wowinapa were pilfering raspberries about six miles northeast of Hutchinson, Minnesota, when they were seen by a farmer, Nathan Lamson, and his son Chauncey. During the brief fire fight that followed, Little Crow was shot and mortally wounded. Nathan Lamson was also wounded in the melee and he and his son became separated during the encounter. Each eventually made it to Hutchinson where they spread the news.

Little Crow's body was found the next day by a search party. Little Crow was wearing clothing taken from a settler he had murdered two days before and his remains were not immediately identified. The body was taken to Hutchinson where it was dismembered. Little Crow's two broken wrists aided in the eventual identification.

Wowinapa escaped the July 3 fight with the Lamsons. He was captured July 28 by U.S. Army troops near Devil's Lake in Dakota Territory and confirmed his father's death. He eventually returned to reservation life and in later years became founder of the YMCA among the Sioux.

Little Crow's grandson became the Reverend John S. Wakeman, pastor of the Yellow Medicine Lutheran Church in Hanley Falls, Minnesota.

JOHN OTHER DAY

In retaliation for Other Day's help to the white population, Sioux raiders burned his farm and destroyed his crops. Eventually rewarded by Congress for his service, he used the $2,500 to buy a farm near Henderson, Minnesota.

ROUND WIND

It is not clear what happened to Round Wind, the Dakota elder whose death sentence was countermanded by President Lincoln. He was not listed as dying or having been released from the prison at Camp McClellan, Iowa, where most prisoners were taken. It is possible that he was sent with a smaller number of others to Crow Creek in Dakota Territory where tribal records for that period have unfortunately been badly damaged. Other than for a letter (below) dictated to his wife while he awaited his scheduled execution, all traces of Round Wind have vanished from history.

> *You know that I did not murder any person and so I*
> *thought I should see you again, but now I shall soon die.*
> *I shall walk in the path of the son of the Great God... I*
> *think I shall now soon be happy in his house so pray much*
> *that you may see me there.*

E.W. EARLE

E.W. survived the devastation of August 18 and the battles at Fort Ridgely and Birch Coulee. He was later reunited with his father, brother, and mother, who survived her captivity by the Sioux.

On his way to the battle at Birch Coulee, he passed the place where his brother, Mrs. Henderson, her two little girls, and Mr. Wedge lay dead and unburied.

In his later life, Earle became a noted physician in Rochester, New York.

LOUIS THIELE

In the days after the fighting ended, Thiele and others set out through the countryside to bury the dead. He eventually worked up the courage to go to the site where his wife and child had been killed. He found their remains mostly eaten by wolves, with little left but bones and fragments of their clothing.

Perhaps out of personal motives — he had knelt beside his slain wife and son and vowed to avenge their deaths — or because he found solace or satisfaction in his service while defending Fort Ridgely, Thiele enlisted in the Union Army. Assigned to Company E, 6th Minnesota Volunteer Infantry, he was posted initially to Fort Snelling for duty along the frontier. During that time he met and later married Fredericke Lunde of St. Paul. With the Civil War still ongoing, his unit was subsequently transferred to Camp Buford, near Helena, Arkansas. From June 1864 until the closing days of the war, the regiment took part in the Mobile, Alabama, campaign.

After the war, Thiele returned to his old homestead near Beaver Falls. He was one of the few to do so. He stayed on the farm only a short time before moving in 1866 into Beaver Falls village. That journey would be the first of several moves that over the years took him to various towns in the area where he established a variety of businesses that included a hotel, several general stores, and a post office.

In 1885, he moved to Fairfax, Minnesota, where, along with one of his sons, he was among the successful petitioners requesting that the village be incorporated. In 1888, when the first village election was held, Louis was elected constable.

Thiele died in 1902 at age 73. He is buried in Fairfax.

MINNIE BUCE CARRIGAN

At Camp Release, Minnie met Louis Thiele who told her that he had buried the five members of her family the Sioux had killed on the first day of the uprising. She was eventually taken to Fort Ridgely and subsequently to St. Peter, passing a deserted and devastated landscape on the way.

A guardian was eventually appointed for her and her siblings, an experience that though not abusive, was less than warm or positive. At age 15, Minnie left to go out on her own, working in summer months and attending school in the winter. In a few years she married, apparently happily, and raised a family of five children. Her recollections of the uprising were written in 1903.

ALEXANDER RAMSEY

Governor of Minnesota through the uprising, Ramsey was re-elected for a second term. He resigned in 1863 to become a United States Senator, serving in that position until 1875. He was later appointed Secretary of War in the cabinet of President Rutherford B. Hayes. Ramsey died in St. Paul in 1903 and is buried in Oakland Cemetery.

Several sites in Minnesota bear his name.

CHARLES FLANDRAU

Recognizing his distinguished service at New Ulm, Governor Ramsey placed Flandrau in charge of the defenses in the south and southwestern portion of the state. He served in that position as a colonel for two years, establishing posts at New Ulm, Garden City, Winnebago, Blue Earth, Martin Lake, and Marysburg. When the war ended he moved briefly to Nevada before returning to Minnesota to practice law. Over the next few years he ran unsuccessfully for governor and chief justice of the Minnesota Supreme Court. In 1870 he left the state permanently to join a law firm in St. Louis where he remained until his death in 1903.

Flandrau State Park and Flandrau, South Dakota, are named in his honor.

SERGEANT JOHN JONES

Jones' adroit handling of Fort Ridgely's artillery was immediately recognized as having played a pivotal role in the fort's defense. He was later commissioned captain of the 3rd Battery, Minnesota Volunteer Artillery, and served on the major expeditions in Dakota Territory led by General Henry Sibley in 1863 and General Alfred Sully in 1864.

LIEUTENANT TIMOTHY SHEEHAN

Promoted to captain in recognition for his exemplary service during the uprising, in December Sheehan and the rest of Company C joined the entire 5th Minnesota Regiment in Mississippi. The regiment was active in the Western Theater until the end of the Civil War, participating in the sieges at Vicksburg, Mississippi, and Spanish Fort and Fort Blakely in Alabama, and the Battle of Tupelo in Mississippi.

Sheehan mustered out of service in September 1865 at Fort Snelling a few days after having been promoted to lieutenant colonel. He returned to his farm near Albert Lea and was later appointed deputy U.S. Marshal. In October 1895, he was wounded during the Battle of Leech Lake, a confrontation usually considered as the last of the Indian uprisings in the continental United States. He spent the remaining years of his life in St. Paul, where he died in 1913.

LIEUTENANT THOMAS GERE

Gere was later promoted to first lieutenant and adjutant in the Fifth Minnesota for his gallantry during the uprising. In his later Civil War service, he was awarded the Medal of Honor for his actions during the Battle of Nashville. He left the army in April 1865 as the war drew to a close.

After the war, Gere began a career with the railroads. He died in 1912 and is buried at Arlington National Cemetery.

MAJOR GENERAL JOHN POPE

Pope had served well in an "orphan" department. Starting without aides, quartermaster, or other staff, he had quelled the major uprisings and managed to stretch his thin forces to protect settlements, escort wagon trains and guard against Confederate guerrillas—all in the face of repeated demands for his troops from national authorities. Far more than most of his contemporaries, he was responsive to civil rights and rather astutely handled civil affairs within his department. Rare among military officers, he sought measures to solve the "Indian problem," not just manage it.

By the time Pope's tour as department commander ended, all but a few Indians had been expelled from the state of Minnesota and relocated 250 miles west. Their forced exodus was in response to the demands of a terrorized public and requests from government officials. Pope's views, by contrast, had shifted considerably over the 29 months he had been in charge. From supporting calls for extermination—fairly common during that period—when he first arrived, by the time he left he was one of the few officials advocating a plan for long-term resolution of the "Indian problem." On February 1, 1865, in his last dispatch as departmental commander, Pope proposed several interesting notions. One called for returning the peaceable bands back east, assisting with food, shelter, and provisions while weaning them away from annuity payments. Warring bands would be promised peace and kind treatment in return for good behavior. Pope was convinced that sales of whiskey and swindles by traders had contributed to the general unrest. Trouble would be greatly reduced, he thought, if the government made it impossible for white men to profit from commerce with Indians. Thus, trade would be regulated, extended only by authorized representatives at specific locations. Officers and soldiers would be prohibited from trading with the tribes.

Pope's sojourn in the Northwest earned him a promotion to brigadier general in the Regular Army. A short time later, on March 13, 1865, he would receive a brevet to major general given in retrospect for his victory over Confederate forces at Island Number 10 three years earlier.

In late 1864, General Grant offered Pope command of a proposed organization that would include the entire former Department of the Northwest plus the states of Kansas and Missouri. The proffer recognized Pope's success in command of the Department of the Northwest as well as changing conditions on the battlefield. Minnesota and portions of Dakota had been generally pacified but new problems had erupted across the Plains in a massive uprising that began in August. Dealing with the issue could be more readily handled by a single commander located closer to the action. The new organization was officially established at St. Louis, Missouri, on January 30, 1865. Pope formally took command five days later.

Pope served in Missouri until October 1, 1866. He later took command of the 3rd Military District performing Reconstruction duty in Georgia, Florida, and Alabama. A series of departmental commands followed: Department of the Lakes (1868); Department of the Missouri (1870); and finally, Department of California and District of the Pacific (1883). On October 26, 1882, he was promoted to major general. He retired from the Army in 1886 after 44 years of service. He died six years later and is buried in Bellefontaine Cemetery in St. Louis.

BRIGADIER GENERAL HENRY SIBLEY

Sibley remained on active duty until August 1866. For the remaining quarter century of his life he was active in business and civic affairs. He served as president of a variety of corporations associated with railroads and financial institutions. His civic endeavors were notable for their number and diversity: president of the chamber of commerce, president of the Minnesota Historical Society, member of the Board of Visitors at the United States Military Academy, president of the Board of Regents of the University of Minnesota, and president of the Board of Indian Commissioners.

Sibley died in St. Paul on February 18, 1891, two days prior to his 80th birthday. He is buried at Oakland Cemetery in that city.

BRIGADIER GENERAL ALFRED SULLY

In the latter stages of the uprising, Sully suggested an unusual peace plan. Believing that much of the Indian problem emanated from unscrupulous traders and agents, he advocated that the military take direct charge of Indian affairs. He believed the large annuity payments intended for the tribes' use provided an incentive for fraud and abuse by the agents and contractors who handled them. Treating the tribes fairly, he thought, would reduce many of the causes for dispute. These views were generally shared by Generals Pope and Sibley. Like those officers also, Sully was frustrated by the presence of British traders who crossed the border and supplied weapons, liquor, and other goods to the Plains tribes.

In 1865, Sully and his troops were slated to assist Colonel Patrick Connor on the Powder River Expedition, an ultimately less than successful campaign against Sioux, Cheyenne, and Arapaho tribesmen in Montana and Dakota Territories. However, public pressure associated with continuing threats against Dakota and Minnesota caused his force to be diverted from the campaign. Sully and a large force were sent instead toward the Devil's Lake region where few hostiles were seen and little was accomplished.

After the so-called Fetterman Massacre—a December 1866 incident not far from present-day Sheridan, Wyoming, in which Captain William J. Fetterman and his 80 men were decoyed into an ambush in which all were slain— Sully chaired a commission that convened to investigate the circumstances surrounding the attack. As events transpired, that would become a familiar role for Sully. His experience as a military commander and his acquaintance with tribes across the central and northern Plains caused him to be called often for duty on special panels. Two years later, he served as commissioner during the talks which ended Red Cloud's War. In the following decade he chaired investigations related to the conflict with the Nez Perce as well.

Sully's Civil War service had earned him brevet promotions to brigadier general and major general in the Regular Army. After the war, he reverted to his permanent grade of lieutenant colonel. He served initially as commander of the 3rd U.S. Infantry. After a subsequent promotion to colonel he assumed command of the 21st U.S. Infantry.

Sully was in command of Fort Vancouver in Washington Territory at the time of his death in 1879. He is buried at Laurel Hill Cemetery in Philadelphia.

REFERENCES

"trader's paper"
Carley, Kenneth, *The Dakota War of 1862*. Minneapolis, MN: Minnesota State Historical Society, 1976, p. 3

"If they are hungry, let them eat grass."
Carley, *The Dakota War of 1862* p. 6

"Storm Lake Massacre"
Michno, Susan J. "Spirit Lake Massacre," *Wild West* Magazine, February 2006
See also
Bristow, David L. "Inkpaduta's Revenge: The True Story of the Storm Lake Massacre," *The Iowan* Magazine, January/February 1999

"friendlies"
Carley, *The Dakota War of 1862*, p. 64

"Bleeding Kansas"
Patrick, E.J., *The Civil War Reader*. New York: MJF Books, 2008 p. 7

"the Sioux became disagreeable and ill-natured…"
Carrigan, Minnie Buce, "Captured by the Indians: Reminiscences of pioneer life in Minnesota," Originally published in *Buffalo Lake News*, January 1903

"Slaughter Slough"
Carley, *The Dakota War of 1862*, p. 23

"We had hardly reached the cornfield when the Indians came…"
Carrigan, Minnie Buce, *Buffalo Lake News*

"I was not strong enough…" (Mary Rieke letter)
Rieke, Reuben D., *Rieke Family Collection.* Lincoln, NE

"During both battles and especially that of the second day..." (George Rieke quote)
Fairfax Centennial, 1882–1982. Fairfax, MN: Booklet published by Centennial Committee Officers and Chairpersons, 1982 p. 42–43

"Thank God, we are all reasonably well..." (George Rieke letter)
Rieke, *Rieke Family Collection*

"...forever beyond the border of the state."
Wingerd, Mary Lethert, *North Country: The Making of Minnesota.* Minneapolis, MN: University of Minnesota Press, 2010 p. 348

"McClellan man"
Phillips, Thomas D., *Boots and Saddles: Military Leaders of the American West,* Caldwell, ID: Caxton Press, 2015, p. 335

"have the right of *habeas corpus*"
Dundy, Judge Elmer J., *United States ex rel. Standing Bear v. Crook,* U.S. District Court, Omaha, Nebraska, 1879

"finest light cavalry in history"
Leckie, Robert, *The Wars of America.* New York: Harper & Row Publishers, 1968, p. 12

"Little Crow was a murderous killer and a cruel master." (August Gluth letter)
Rieke, *Rieke Family Collection*

"You know that I did not murder anyone." (Round Wind letter)
Brown, Curt. "A Late Reprieve Saved Dakota Elder," *Minneapolis Star Tribune,* August 26, 2017, p. B4

"Indian problem"
Phillips, *Boots and Saddles: Military Leaders of the American West,* p. 307

BIBLIOGRAPHY

Books

Berg, Scott W., *38 Nooses: Lincoln, Little Crow, and the Beginning of the Frontier's End,* New York: Random House LLC, 2012

Bryant, Charles S., *History of the Minnesota Valley and History of the Sioux Massacre,* Minneapolis, MN: North Star Publishing Company, 1882

Carley, Kenneth, *The Dakota War of 1862,* Minneapolis, MN: Minnesota State Historical Society, 1976

Christgau, John, *Birch Coulee: The Epic Battle of the Dakota War,* Lincoln, NE: Bison Books, 2012

Clodfelter, Michael, *The Dakota War: The United States Army versus the Sioux, 1862–1865,* Jefferson, NC: McFarland Co. Publishers, 2006

Cox, Hank H., *Lincoln and the Sioux Uprising of 1862,* Nashville, TN: Cumberland House Publishing, 2005

Cozzens, Peter, *General John Pope: A Life for the Nation,* Champaign-Urbana, IL: University of Illinois Press, 2000

Eicher, John H. and David J. Eicher, *Civil War High Commands,* Stanford, CA: Stanford University Press, 2001

Ellis. Richard M., *General Pope and U.S. Indian Policy,* Albuquerque, NM: University of New Mexico Press, 1978

Hutton, Paul A., *Soldiers West: Biographies from the Military Frontier,* Lincoln, NE: University of Nebraska Press, 1987

Johnson, Roy P., *The Siege of Fort Abercrombie,* Bismarck, ND: Historical Society of North Dakota, 1957

Jones, Evan, *The Minnesota, Forgotten River*, New York: Holt Rinehart, 1962

Klein, Janet and Joyce Kloncz (eds), *Family and Friends of Dakota Uprising* (Volumes I and II).Renville County Historical Society, 2012. Material provided courtesy of Nancy Rieke Gulbranson

McDermott, John D., *A Guide to the Indian Wars of the West*, Lincoln, NE and London: University of Nebraska Press, 1998

Michno, Gregory F., *Dakota Dawn: The Decisive First Week in the Sioux Uprising, August 1862*, El Dorado Hills, CA: Savas Beatie, 2011

— *Encyclopedia of Indian Wars*, Missoula, MT: Mountain Press Publishing Company, 2003

Neil, Rev. Edward D., *History of the Minnesota Valley*, Minneapolis, MN: North Star Publishing Company, 1882

Phillips, Thomas D., *Boots and Saddles: Military Leaders of the American West*, Caldwell, ID. Caxton Press, 2015

Rieke, George, *Gedichte*, selected and edited by G.E. Miller, copyright A.V. Rieke, Minneapolis, MN, 1927

Rieke, Robert W., *History of the Minnesota Riekes*, copyright Robert Rieke, Charlotte, NC 1992

Sully, Langdon, *No Tears for the General: The Life of Alfred Sully, 1821–1879*, Palo Alto: CA: American West Publishing Co., 1974

Utley, Robert et al, *Indian Wars*, New York: Mariner Books, 2002

Wagner, Margaret E., Gary W. Gallagher, Paul Finkelman (eds), *The Library of Congress Civil War Desk Reference*, New York: Simon & Schuster, 2002

Warner, Ezra J., *Generals in Blue: Lives of the Union Army Commanders*, Baton Rouge, LA: Louisiana State University Press, 1964

Wellman, Paul I., *The Indian Wars of the West*, Garden City, NY: Doubleday & Company, 1956

Newspapers

Fairfax (Minnesota) Standard-Gazette
Earle, E.W., "Reminiscences: 140th Anniversary of the U.S.-Dakota War

of 1862," August 21, August 28, September 4, September 11, September 18, 2002

Minneapolis Star Tribune
Brown, Curt, "A Late Reprieve Saved Dakota Elder," August 26, 2017, p. B4. Material provided courtesy of Nancy Rieke Gulbranson

Magazines

Indian Country Today
Schilling, Vincent, "The Traumatic True History and Name List of the Dakota 38," December 27, 2017

Minnesota History
Kane, Lucille A., "The Sioux Treaties and the Traders," June 1951

North Dakota History
Danziger, Edmund J., Jr., "The Crow Creek Experiment: An Aftermath of the Sioux War," Spring 1970
Johnson, Roy P., "The Sioux at Fort Abercrombie," January 1957
Pfaller, Louis, "Sully's Expedition of 1864," January 1974

The Iowan
Bristow, David L., "Inkpaduta's Revenge: The True Story of the Storm Lake Massacre," January/February 1999

Wild West
Kennan, Jerry, "The Battle of Whitestone Hill," June 2008
Michno, Susan J., "Spirit Lake Massacre," February 2006

Pamphlets

Buffalo Lake News
"Captured by the Indians: Reminiscences of pioneer life in Minnesota." Carrigan, Minnie Buce. Originally published in January 1903

Fort Ridgely: A Journey to the Past
Minnesota State Historical Society

Fairfax Centennial, 1882–1982
Centennial Committee Publication Fairfax, Minnesota 1982

Websites

Biographical Data of the United States Congress
Henry Hastings Sibley
http:bioguide.congress.gov/scripts/biodisplay.p1?index=S000396
Retrieved July 21, 2013

The U.S. Army and the Sioux—Part 2: Battle of the Badlands
National Park Service
http: www.nps.gov/thro/historyculture/the-us-army-and-the-sioux-part-2.htm
Retrieved November 8, 2017

ABOUT THE AUTHORS

A native Minnesotan, REUBEN D. RIEKE developed an abiding interest in the state's history and in his family's involvement in the Sioux Uprising of 1862. Stories of hazardous flights to safety, bitter combat at Fort Ridgely, captivity at the hands of the Sioux, and daring escapes left an unquenchable thirst for knowledge about this fascinating period along America's frontier.

After graduating from high school at Fairfax, Reuben attended the University of Minnesota-Minneapolis, majoring in chemistry. He then went on for graduate studies at the University of Wisconsin-Madison, receiving a Doctor of Philosophy degree in organic chemistry. After a year of postdoctoral studies at the University of California-Los Angeles, he began is teaching career at the University of North Carolina-Chapel Hill where he became a full professor. He then returned to the Midwest, spending 27 years at the University of Nebraska-Lincoln, teaching organic chemistry and carrying out a major research program.

Known worldwide for his scientific contributions in the area of organometallic chemistry, Dr. Rieke has been honored in his home state by being placed on the University of Minnesota's Wall of Honor. In 2001, he received the University's Outstanding Achievement Award. He has published more than 220 peer reviewed scientific publications and has been awarded 25 patents. He is the author of the 2017 book *Chemical Synthesis Using Highly Reactive Metals*, published by John Wiley and Sons. In August, 2018 Dr. Rieke was awarded the Albert Nelson Marquis Lifetime Achievement Award.

Reuben and his wife Loretta reside in Lincoln, Nebraska, where he continues to write about chemistry and the history of southern Minnesota.

During a 36-year career in the military, TOM PHILLIPS led an isolated unit through a terrorist episode, ran a think tank for the Commander-in-Chief Strategic Air Command, served as Director of the Air Force Personnel Readiness Center during Operation Desert Storm, and led some of the first American troops into Sarajevo, Bosnia-Herzegovina. He is believed to be the only Air Force officer to graduate at the top of his class from Officer Training School, Squadron Officer School, and Air Command and Staff College.

Following his military career, Phillips worked as a university administrator before beginning a full-time writing career. His most recent works include *In the Shadows of Victory: America's Forgotten Military Leaders, 1776–1876* and *In the Shadows of Victory II: America's Forgotten Military Leaders, The Spanish-American War to World War II.* He teaches courses on Americana and military history for the Osher Life Long Learning Institute at the University of Nebraska-Lincoln. Tom is a graduate of Air Command and Staff College and Air War College and has degrees from Colorado State University and the University of Colorado. He is a member of Phi Kappa Phi National Scholastic Honorary Society.

He and his wife Nita live in Lincoln, Nebraska, where he writes about military history and baseball.

INDEX

Military organizations, listed alphabetically

General index

HELLGATEPRESS.COM

www.ingramcontent.com/pod-product-compliance
Lightning Source LLC
Chambersburg PA
CBHW051952090426
42741CB00008B/1368